AF541751

ENVIRONMENTAL IMPACT OF INDUSTRIES ON SUBURBAN ENVIRONMENTS

Environmental Impact of Industries on Suburban Environments

Professor S. A. Abbasi
PhD, DSc, FIPHE, FIE

Director
Centre for Pollution Control and Biowaste Energy
Pondicherry (Central) University, Kalapet, Pondicherry—605 014

and

Dr. S. Vinithan
M.Sc., Ph.D.

Scientist
Centre for Pollution Control and Biowaste Energy
Pondicherry (Central) University, Kalapet, Pondicherry—605 014

1997

DISCOVERY PUBLISHING HOUSE
NEW DELHI—110 002

Published by :

Discovery Publishing House
4831/24, Ansari Road, Prahlad Street
Darya Ganj, New Delhi—110 002 (INDIA)
Phone : 327 92 45
Fax : 91-11-3253475

First Published—1997

ISBN 81-7141-397-8 (set)

Laser Typeset by :

Allied Computers
Karnal (Haryana)

Printed at : **Tarun Offset** !

Dedicated to

Neelofer *Didi,* **Sofia** *Aapa* **and**
Rabi *Behen*

—S.A. Abbasi

Pappa **Shri Sethumadhavan Nair** *and*
Mummy **Smt. Leelavathy**

—S. Vinithan

Contents

Preface

In the modern competitive world of open economies no region can survive without extensive industrialization. At the same time if industries grow at the cost of environmental quality the very purpose of industrialization as an instrument of progress and well-being can be defeated.

Fortunately know-how is available, right here in India, to conduct sophisticated environmental impact assessment studies for diagnosing environmental problems caused by industrialization. Technology is also available to treat any type of industrial waste and to make the industries environment friendly. All we need is a collective will to utilize the available know-how for marshalling our progress in harmony with the environment.

We had an opportunity to demonstrate the power and sophistication of the Indian know-how when we were asked to conduct regional environmental impact assessment and sustainability studies, first by Government of Tamil Nadu (in Manali, Chennai) and then by Government of Pondicherry (in Pillayarkuppam-Kirumampakkam). Both the studies were the first of their type in the respective States, indeed two among the very few done anywhere in India.

This book which presents a typical regional EIA study, with specific reference to an industrialized pocket of Pondicherry, may serve as a model for others to follow and improve.

The book may provide a useful study material for the students of environmental science and environmental engineering. There are a few text-books on EIA available in the market but detailed case-studies which may enable the students to appreciate the real-life problems are not available.

We are thankful to Mr. Vasant Arul Akala and Ms. Debarati Bardhan who, along with us, led field teams in conducting this study. It was a pleasure to work with them and that association is now a very sweet memory.

We are thankful to Government of Pondicherry; in particular Dr. Balasubramanian, Director, DSTE and Shri C.V. Srinivasan, Chief Town Planner, for commissioning this study and helping us in conducting it.

S.A. Abbasi
S. Vinithan

1 Introduction

The union territory of Pondicherry, India, has witnessed rapid industrialisation over the past one and half decades. This has brought about economic prosperity but has also stressed the environment of the territory and, in some areas, adversely affected the quality of the life of its citizens.

Pillayarkuppam-Kirumampakkam area, which constitutes one of the four major industrialised pockets in Pondicherry has witnessed an outburst of industrial growth over the past one and half decades. This area comprises of large and medium scale industries situated close to small-scale industries in the PIPDIC (Pondicherry Industrial Promotion Development and Investment Corporation) estate. Just outside the peripheries of industrial campuses, and sometimes interspersed between industries are residential, sensitive, and agricultural areas (Figure 1). There have been strident complaints from the residents of the area about the deteriorating state of the environment. This had made it imperative that the status of the environment of the Pillayarkuppam-Kirumampakkam area be evaluated. This study was therefore undertaken for a total EIA, encompassing all aspects of the physical and biological environment *viz* air, water, land and solid wastes to assess the impact of industrialization on the environment and seek answers to the following questions:-

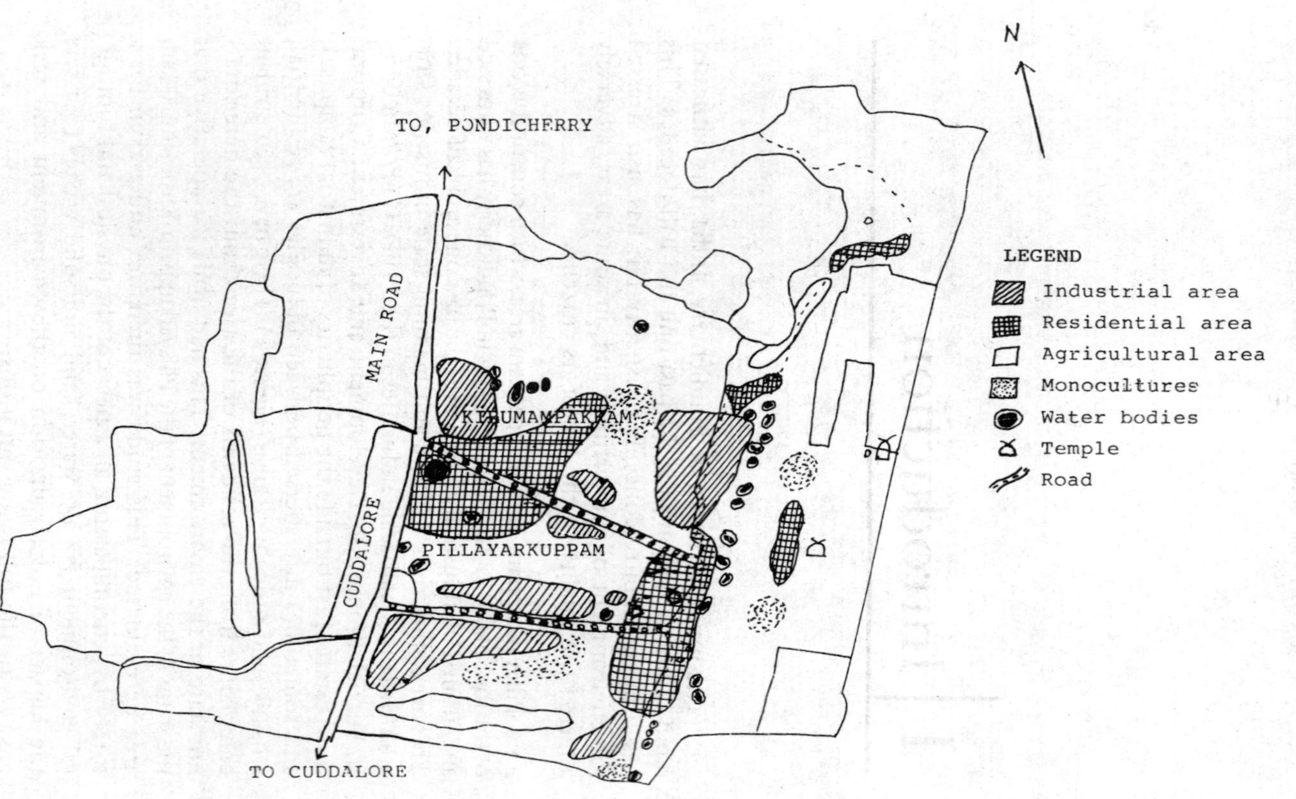

Figure 1. Land-use Map

i) What is the extent of environmental impacts of the existing industries?

ii) Is further industrialisation expansion sustainable in the area?

iii) What are the steps needed to make the existing development (and future development, if any) sustainable ?

Need and Relevance of the Study

EIA (Environmental Impact Assessment) forms the basis for immediate management plans and models (Abbasi & Arya, 1996). Under the current industrial development of the union territory of Pondicherry, India, Pillayarkuppam-Kirumampakkam area is earmarked as a potential zone of industrial growth and expansion.

The industrial estate of Pillayarkuppam-Kirumampakkam is now only a relic of its healthy past. Falling within the taluk of Bahour (control area selected for the present study), this area too saw its share of good agriculture and justly formed a part of the "Bread Basket of Pondicherry". As the area was blessed with good and abundant ground and surface water, agricultural activities was the main occupation and source of income for the inhabitants. Good soil, good water contributed positively towards a very good crop yield. Hence, the present Pillayarkuppam-Kirumampakkam industrial area was then green with large fields of fine quality paddy (*Oryza sativa*), groundnut (*Arachis hypogia*), sugar cane (*Saccharum officinalum*), cotton (*Gosippium sp.*), ragi (*Eleucine coracane*) and millet (*Panicum sp.*). Undoubtedly, with agriculture being most favoured in this area, most of the inhabitants were farmers.

With the advent of small-scale industries in the area, agriculture suffered a slight setback. Lured by monitory gains the small-time farmers sold the lands to more and more entrepreneurs. With this sudden boom in industries, the pattern of resource utilization in the form of energy, water usage, *etc* increased drastically leading to the inevitable resource disturbance and imbalance.

From this, the scenario gradually worsened. With over-utilization/exploitation of ground water, salt water intrusion occured increasingly rendering the ground water unutilizable. Regular inflow of industrial effluents into the ponds disturbed their ecological equilibrium. Consequently, the water which previously could be used for domestic and agricultural purposes, became exceedingly unusable. Salinity rendered the soil unfit for agriculture. This was clearly evident by a change in the cropping pattern. Sugarcane cultivation was wiped out completely and there was 90% reduction in the groundnut cultivation and about 80% decrease in ragi and hybrid millet cultivation. Only paddy continued to be grown (which is comparatively resistant to salinity), that too with diminishing yields.

Today, the land bears no resemblance to its past, except for a few scattered cotton or ragi fields and a few patches of paddy. Added to this, is the inclusion, in recent years, of large tracts of land under monocultures of *Casuarina equisetifolia*, banana (*Musa sp.*), and coconut (*Cocus nucifera*) etc.

Good quality water is now an scarce commodity in this area. With the need for water increasing exponentially, pollution of the present water resources is effecting the inhabitants of Pillayarkuppam-Kirumampakkam to such an extent that water for drinking and domestic purposes is being transported into the village from other areas. Even industries are pretreating their water prior to utilization.

The quality of the air is also equally affected. A pungent and nauseating smell pervades.

One freely comes across piles of solid wastes dumped here and there in the Pillayarkuppam-Kirumampakkam area. These dumpings are not only a major environmental hazard but are also objectionable from a purely civic point of view, because they are unloaded either on government-owned land or private property. These may also cause ground water pollution by percolating to the ground water table thereby affecting the ground water aquifer.

Moreover no such quantification of the air and water quality, studies on land, and studies on impact of solid waste dumps on spatial and temporal scale had been done before, except routine surveys done by the industries themselves.

Objectives of the Study

In compliance with the need and relevance of the study afore mentioned, the objective for the study were set as below.

a) to study the present ambient air quality with respect to particulates (SPM) and gases (NO_x, SO_2, Cl_2, H_2S and H_2SO_4).

b) to study various water quality parameters for both ground and surface water to assess the extent of water pollution in the area.

c) to assess the impact on land-use especially on agriculture.

d) to collect appropriate agricultural data for evaluating the changes that have taken place for the past ten years in various agricultural activities.

e) to assess the impact of solid waste dumps on the ground and surface water resources.

f) to study the charecteristics of solid waste leachates and their effects.

The Study Area

Salient features of the study area are presented below :

Location	:	13 Km south of Pondicherry
	:	6 Km north of Cuddalore
Size	:	3.5 Km²
Temperature and rainfall		
Average annual temperature		
maximum	:	32°c
minimum	:	27°c
Average annual relative humidity	:	62%
Average annual rainfall	:	900 mm
Topography and drainage	:	Plains with no evident drainage patterns (water stagnation is evident)
Infrastructure	:	Telecommunication link up with Pondicherry and Cuddalore, India.

Road route	:	East coastroad NH.
Power supply	:	Main grid
Major industries		
Number	:	Approximately 20.
Type	:	Metallurgical, paper and pulp, Chemical and service industries (Table 1 and Figure 2)
Air	:	Laden with a characteristic persistent odour
Water		
Primary Source (Irrespective of usage)	:	Ground water
Number of surface water bodies	:	12
Approximate volume of a surface water body	:	2000 m
Land-use (Figure 3)		
Percentage of land under industrialization	:	40
Percentage of land under agriculture	:	10
Percentage of land under monoculture	:	25
Percentage of land under natural vegetation	:	10
Percentage of residential land	:	15
Socio-economic		
Employment	:	Average one person per family
Average per capita income	:	Rs 1100 - 1500
Average literacy	:	Primary level
Population Density		
1981	:	~ 6,000
1991	:	~ 8,000
Permanent residents	:	~ 5,000
Floating residents	:	~ 2,500

Table 1. List of Industries

Sl. No.	*Name of Industry*
1.	East Coast Steel
2.	Maharaja Modern Rice Mill
3.	United Abrasives Limited
4.	Pondicherry Papers Limited
5.	Parry Engineering Limited
6.	Neycer India Limited
7.	Silcal Industries Limited
8.	Pondy Allingment and Allied Products (P) Limited
9.	JBF Synthetic Industries Limited
10.	Elfotech
11.	Mowbry's Metals
12.	PYG Organics
13.	Metal Alloys Ltd
14.	Jasco
15.	Supreme Aromatics
16.	Pondy Leather
17.	Ganga Varnish
18.	Metal Industries Limited
19.	Uday Kumar Ltd
20.	Mittal Ispat Ltd
21.	Sharda Castings
22.	Pondy Rolling Mills

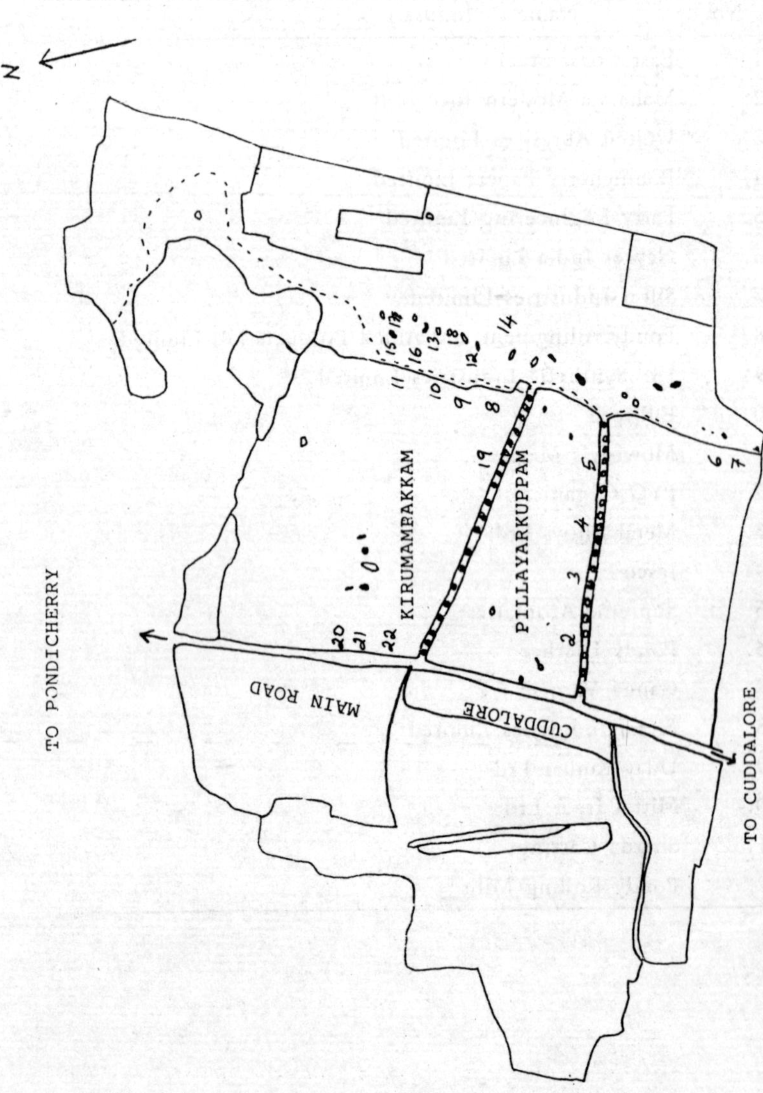

Figure 2. Industrial locations in the study area. (the numbers refers to the serial numbers and

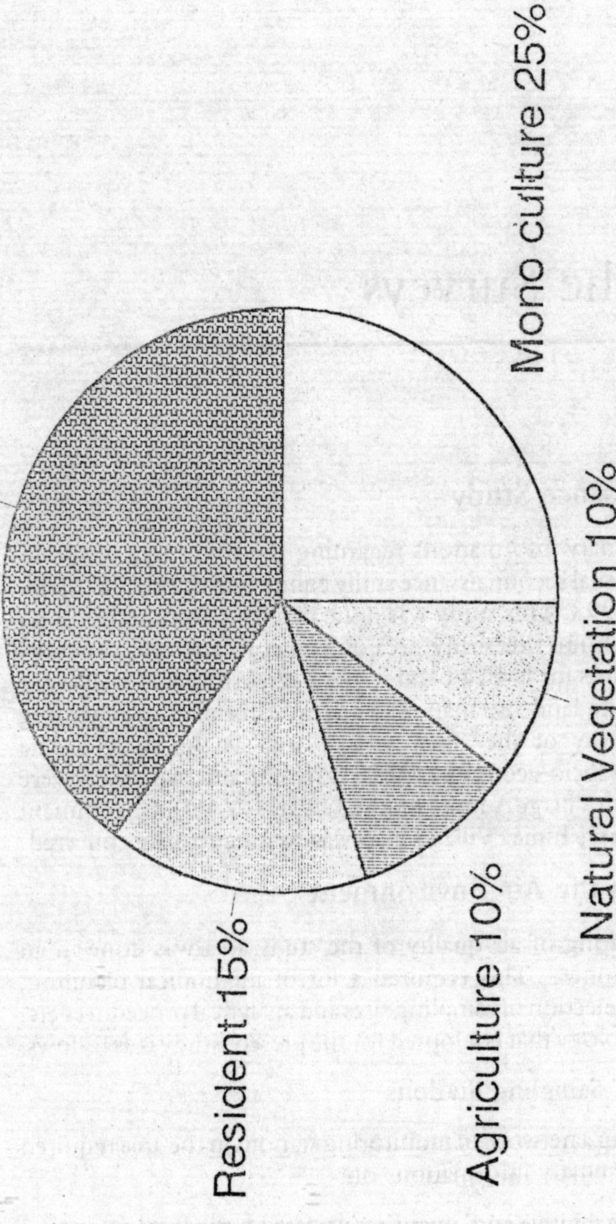

Figure 3. LAND-USAGE

2 The Surveys

Reconnaissance Study

Preliminary informations regarding the study area were obtained by a visual reconnaissance study conducted during October–November 1993. This study was done mainly to have a thorough knowledge about the study area and also to identify potential sampling points for both air and water quality studies as well as for developing the land-use map of the area. Informations regarding the past history of the study area as well as the current data pertaining to socio-economic status, agricultural activities, *etc* were collected from Village Administrative Officers (VAO), Government of Pondicherry, India. Village map was simultaneously collected.

Studies on the Air Environment

Monitoring of air quality of the study area was done in an extensive manner. This required a lot of methodical planning, appropriate selection of sampling sites and analytical procedures *etc.* The methodology that is adopted for the present study is as follows.

Selection of Sampling Stations

Planning a network of monitoring stations in the area required a lot of preliminary informations on:

a) qualitative and quantitative data on the local sources of air pollution.

b) topography

c) population distribution

d) land-use pattern and

e) climatology

In pursuance of the above, information on type of industries, their process flows (included raw materials used and their quantity, the main processes involved, final products and its quantity, emission *etc*) and stack condition were obtained from the records of Department of Science and Technology (DSTE), Government of Pondicherry, India. A visual reconnaissance study conducted during October-November 1993 formed the base. It outlined the necessity of a study in the area apart from defining to a large extent the sampling sites. The land-use map also proved to be very useful. Population distribution in the area was studied in order to identify the potential receptor sites. Climatological data was to an extent available from DSTE, major source being the Indian Meteorological Department at Pune, India, as well as Madras, India, and the French Institute, Pondicherry, India. The meteorological station at Cuddalore, Tamil Nadu, India, proved very handy in developing the pattern of wind conditions and thereby helping us to decide the priority sampling sites, lest we loose the particular conditions at that particular time of the year.

More important though not significant was information collected on the influence of extraneous sources on air quality of Pillayarkuppam-Kirumampakkam. Though marginal in scale it would be very apt to mention here that industrial sites located in the neighbouring town/village do contribute to pollution loads in the study area. This is based on the prevalent odour in the air and heresay.

Location of Sampling Sites

Principal factors which governed the location of sampling sites were the objectives, the particular method or instrument used for sampling, resources available, physical access and security against loss and tampering.

Based on the objectives, location sites were placed close to receptor sites (human settlements, agricultural fields, monocultures *etc*) in order to estimate the damage or effects on human health and materials. Critical areas such as hospitals, schools, prime residential areas were also covered so as to fulfil this objective. At the same time, sites upwind and downwind of sources were identified in order to assess the contribution from specific sources. Topographical and micrometeorological information were of much use in this case. Since the sources of pollution were treated as an 'area source', samplers were placed so as to cover the whole study area.

Location of the monitoring stations, were also determined by the following criteria:

a) Representativeness

A representative sampling site reflects the concentration and fluctuations of air pollutants within the area. Therefore, care was taken to place the sites away from:

i) nearby sources of air pollution like domestic chimneys and houses where wood, charcoal, *etc* were used as fuel. Samplers were placed at least 25 meters away from such sources

ii) absorbing surfaces (foliage, walls *etc*)

iii) areas where considerable land - use changes were going to occur(e.g. construction, monoculture plantings *etc*.)

iv) sampling sites also ensured representativeness of population movements.

(b) Compatability

In order to compare air quality data from different sites, the details of each location were standardized, i.e.

i) all samplers were placed at least four meters above the ground and two to three meters from vertical and horizontal surfaces.

ii) technicalities with respect to method, operation, *etc* were same for all samplers.

(c) Physical Requirements

Monitoring sites fulfilled the following conditions:

i) it was available for the full duration of sampling.

ii) it was accessible for 24 hours.

iii) electrical power of sufficient rating was available.

iv) it was vandal-proof.

(d) Topographical and Meteorological Conditions

The land-use plan of the area shows the various topographical features which may affect the local meteorological conditions. No such special features (tall buildings, mountains, valley *etc*) exist which may bring about drastic changes in the local meteorology except for the land-sea breeze circulation which dominate and change the local wind pattern. The distance of penetration would determine the dispersion and transport of pollutants.

Sampling Stations

As mentioned earlier the industries in this area are very close to potential receptor sites. Therefore it was very difficult to designate or categorize the location into industrial, residential, and sensitive areas, as promulgated by Central Pollution Control Board (CPCB). Moreover,no such core or buffer areas/zones exist in this area. Nevertheless, based on the objectives to be achieved, nature of and effects on receptors, distance between the receptors and industries, and the above mentioned facts, potential sampling stations were established (Figure 1). The stations represented.

a) Industrial location : This was at PIPDIC's industrial estate.

b) Sensitive area : A primary school.

c) Residential area : Three locations were studied on the basis of predominant wind directions.

d) Control area : This was at Bahour (a near by village to the study area) and identical in its setting to the study area but free from the impact of industrial pollution.

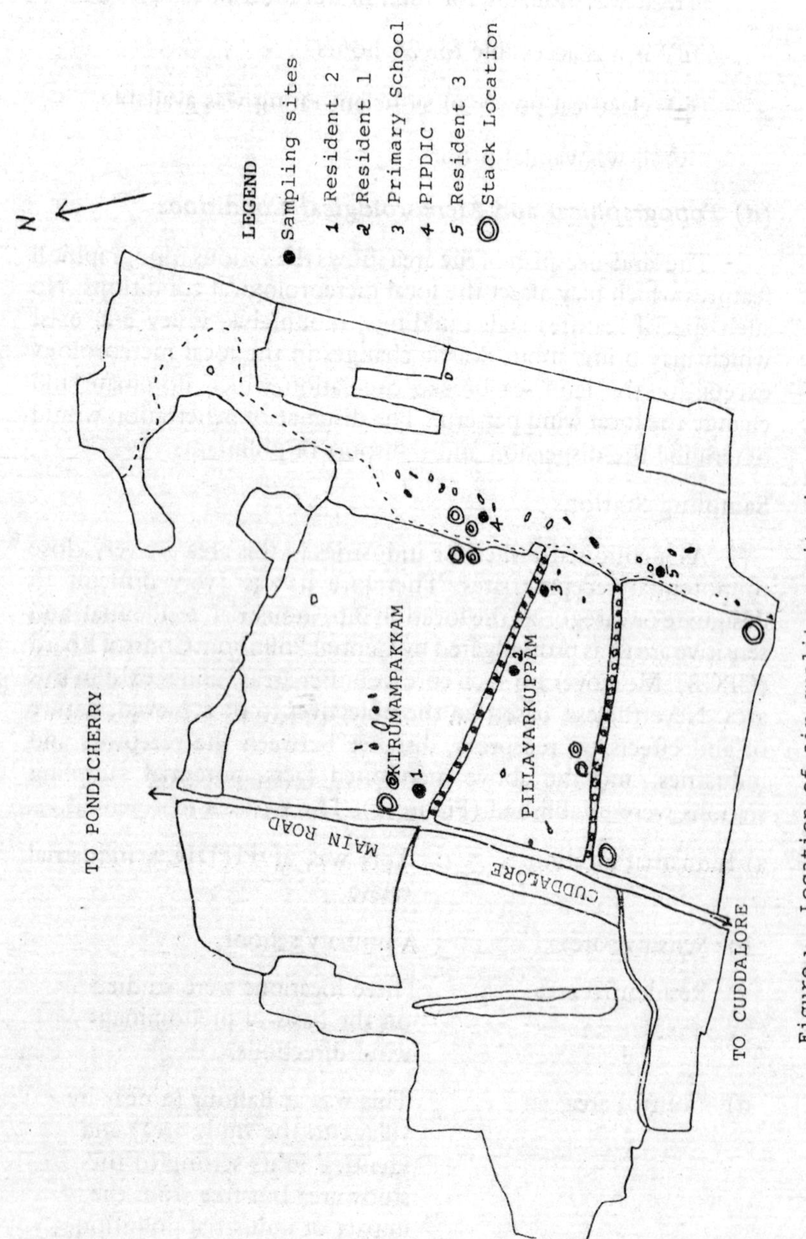

Figure 1. Location of air quality monitoring stations

Thus six sampling stations were established for extensive monitoring of the air quality of the study area.

Period, Frequency and Duration of Sampling

The period, frequency and duration of sampling were appropriate to the objectives of the study. Meteorological and source emission factors which influence the atmospheric concentration (Peavy *et al*, 1986) were taken into account. Factors primarily determining the same such as wind direction in different seasons, diurnal variation of wind speed, and other stability parameters (council of Environmental Quality, 1982) were considered. Other important determinants were such that measurable quantities of pollutants were trapped at the end of the sampling period to obtain statistically reliable averages over the duration of sampling.

Over all 5,472 hours of sampling at 8 hour continuous stretches were done covering more than 800 air quality parameter values across 12 months. Samplings were conducted during days as well as nights.

Meteorology

In an area like Pillayarkuppam-Kirumampakkam, where industries and residents are so closely placed (as shown in the land-use map) it becomes very important to study the meteorological conditions, especially with reference to receiver effects, apart from serving other important objectives. Since these areas come on the coast, where the atmosphere is turbulent, stability of the atmosphere would determine the dispersion and fate of pollutants (Battan, 1979; Byers, 1974).

In order to achieve the above, meteorological studies under parameters like temperature, relative humidity, wind speed and wind direction were carried out during the period of study. Wind roses for the study area were simultaneously generated (Figs. 2–7).

Equipment

Maximum and Minimum Thermometer, Relative Humidity Meter (Hygrometer), Wind Vane, Automated Anemometer.

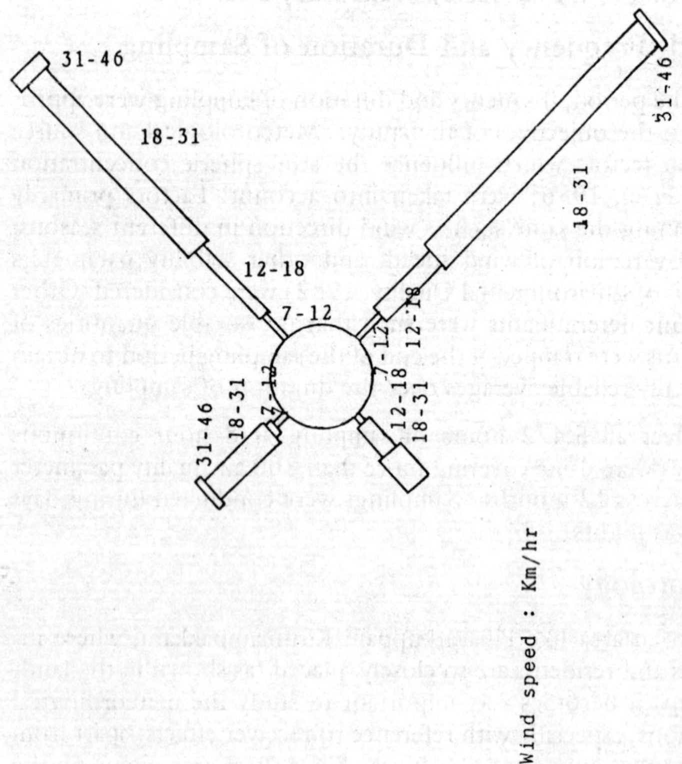

Figure 2. Wind rose March - June 48 hr av

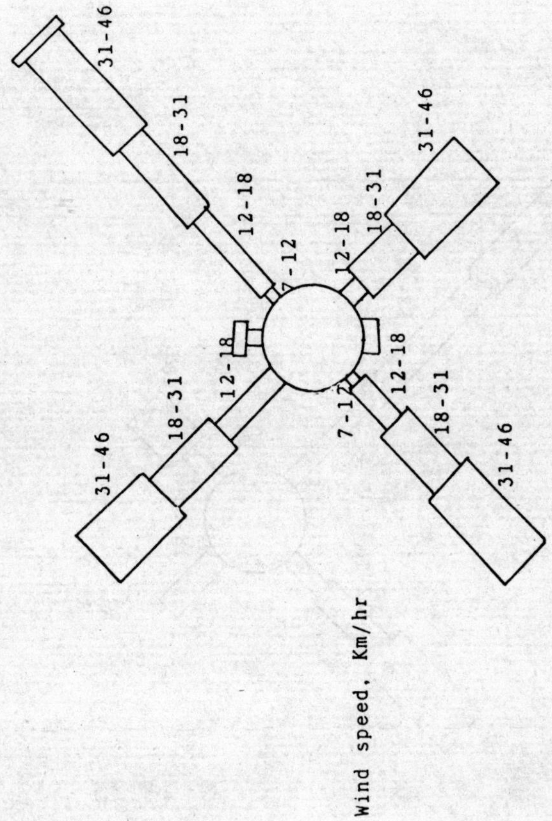

Figure 3. Wind rose July-November, 48 hr av

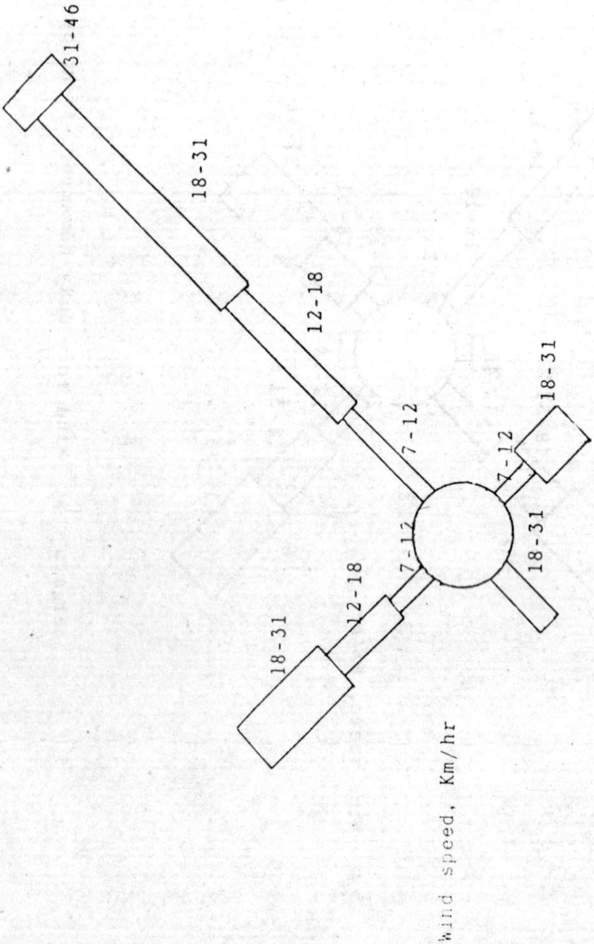

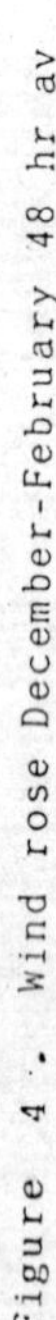

Figure 4 . Wind rose December-February 48 hr av

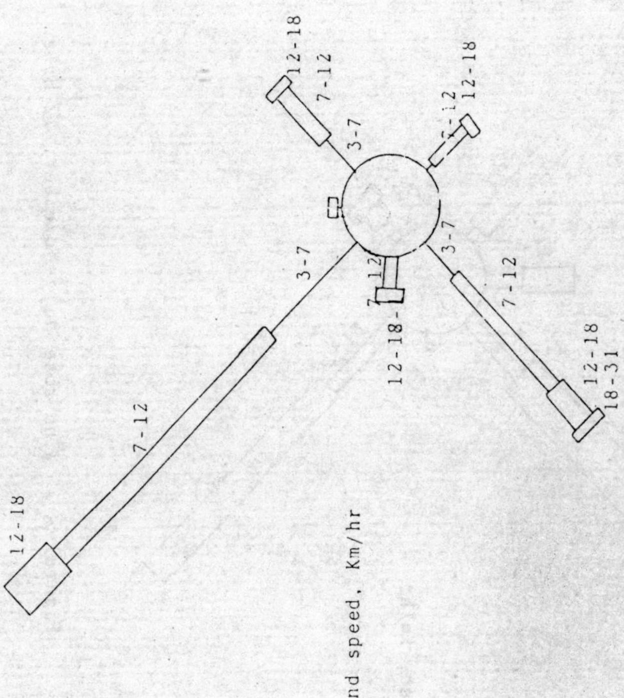

Figure 5. Wind rose March-June, 12 hr av

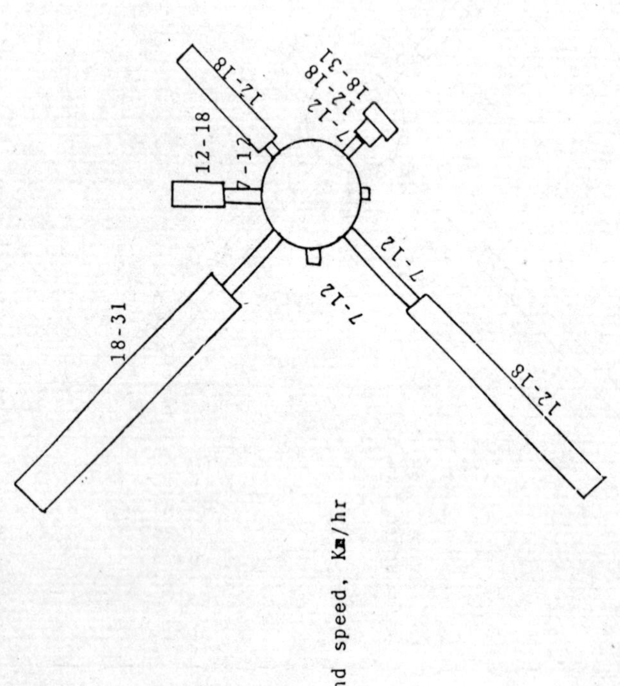

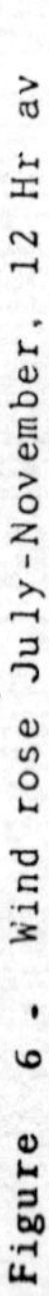

Figure 6 - Wind rose July-November, 12 Hr av

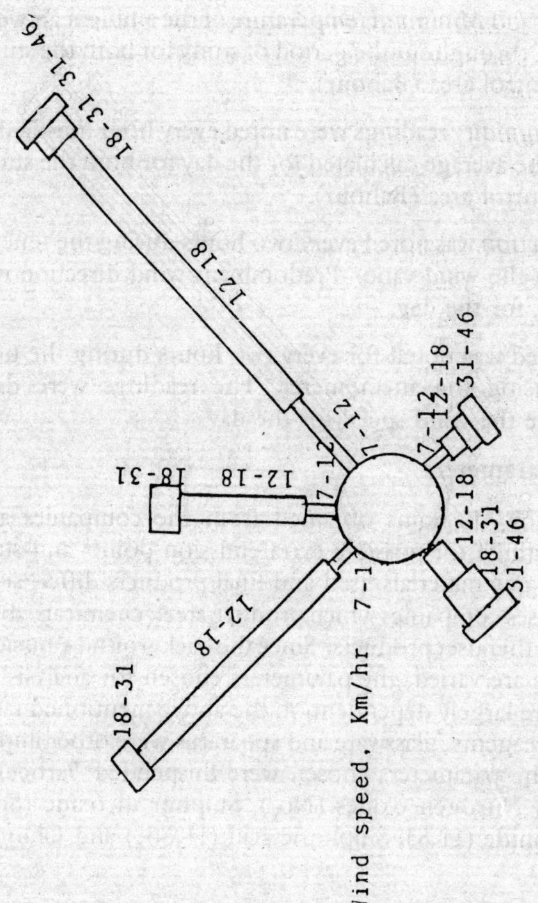

Figure 7. Wind rose December-February, 12 hr av

Method

Maximum and Minimum temperature of the ambient air were noted every day, throughout the period of study for both the study area and the control area (Bahour).

Relative humidity readings were noted every hour during day and night and the average calculated for the day for both the study area and the control area (Bahour).

Wind direction was noted every two hours during the time of sampling, using the wind vane. Predominant wind direction was then calculated, for the day.

Wind Speed was noted for every two hours during the time of sampling, using the anemometer. The readings were then averaged to give the wind speed for the day.

Selection of Parameters

Process flow diagrams obtained from the companies and DSTE were scanned for possible extra emission points and stack emissions. The raw materials used and final products differ, since the area comprises companies which produce steel, chemicals, dyes, varnishes, and other user products. Since the background emissions from industries are varied, the parameters chosen for analysis for ambient air were largely dependent on the above mentioned facts. Availability of reagents, glassware and apparatus were other important factors. The parameters chosen were Suspended Particulate Matter (SPM), Nitrogen oxides (No_x), Sulphur di oxide (So_2), Hydrogen sulphide (H_2S), Sulphuric acid (H_2So_4) and Chlorine (Cl_2).

Sampling and Analysis of Particulates and Gases

It would be apt to mention that like in any other industrial area, apart from the industries, secondary sources such as transport, burning of domestic fuel do contribute to local pollution load (Peavy *et al*, 1986; Stern *et al*,1973 and Institute for air pollution training, 1975). Therefore, it becomes very difficult as such to estimate pollution loads caused by industries alone. In order to minimize influence of such extraneous factors into our estimation, care was taken to keep the samplers away from such sources, as mentioned earlier.

Micrometeorological conditions vary from season to season and even day to day (Battan, 1979). Diurnal variation in the atmospheric condition due to industrial activities also takes place. Hence sampling was conducted during various seasons as well as during days and nights. This procedure was adopted under the assumption that industries do carry their full operation and production even during the night time.

For the present study extensive monitoring of air quality of the study area was done for one year. Sampling was done during February-April 1994, June and October 1994, and January 1995.

Materials

Materials used for various analytical purpose were as follows:

Reagents

Analytical grade reagents were used. Assay of most of the chemicals were above 95%. Impurities, if any, in the reagents were removed by way of interferences removal technique. Chemicals used are mentioned while explaining the various methods adopted for the estimation of different water quality parameters under study, which is given in the forthcoming paragraph under Methods.

Plasticware and glassware

The plasticware employed were made of high quality temperature resistant and scratch proof materials. The materials used were also odour free. Glassware used were made of alkali and temperature resistant material (Corning/Borosil make).

Equipment

Equipment used for the analytical work include:

(i) High volume samplers (Envirotech, APM415) with gas monitoring kits

(ii) Visible spectrophotometer (Systronics)

(iii) BOD Incubator (Gambaks-106)

(iv) High precision (0.001 gms) Anamed monopan weighing balance

(v) Whatman (FIA) glass fibre filter papers.

Analytical Methods

Many methods exist for the sampling and analysis of ambient particulates and gases. For sampling and analysis, internationally accepted methods as documented in the treatizes of APHA (1977), were employed. Final concentrations were compared with the standards of air quality prescribed by regulatory agencies CPCB (Central Pollution Control Board) and Ministry Of Environment (MOEn), New Delhi, India. Other important factors taken into consideration were: range, sensitivity of the method, precision, accuracy, stability, interferences, feasibility and availabilty of infra-structure *etc* as enlisted in Table 2.1. Thus meticulous quality control was done to ensure the authenticity of the data.

Estimation of Suspended Particulates (SPM)

Air was drawn into a covered housing and through a filter by means of high volume air sampler to an average flow rate of 1.5 m^3/min. This allowed collection of suspended particles having diameter of less than 100 micron on the glass fibre filter paper. The mass concentration (m g/Nm^3) of suspended particulates in the ambient air was computed by measuring the mass of collected particulates and the volume of air sampled.

Estimation of Nitrogen Oxides (No_x)

Oxides of nitrogen were collected by bubbling air at the rate of 1.5 litres/min through a sodium hydroxide solution to form a stable solution of sodium nitrate. The nitrate ion produced during sampling, was determined colorimetrically by reacting the exposed absorbing reagent with hydrogen peroxide, sulphanilamide, and N(1-naphthyl) ethylenediamine dihydrochloride (NEDA). A calibration curve for the above had already been prepared.

Estimation of Sulphur Dioxide (So_2)

Sulphur dioxide from the air stream was absorbed in a sodium tetra-chloromercurate solution to form stable dichlorosulphitomercurate. The amount of sulphur dioxide was then estimated by the colour produced when P-rosaniline hydrochloride was added to the solution. The colour was estimated by reading from a spectrophotom-

Table 2.1. Criteria Used for the Methods Chosen

Sl. No.	Parameters	Method Chosen	Range & Sensitivity	Precision/Accuracy Stability	Interferences	Feasibility	Remark
1.	Particulates	Gravimetric	1mg/m^3 to very high concentration(dependant on flow rate and average timing).	Repeatability 3% Reproductibility 3.7%Accuracy dependant on flow rate.the filter.	Particulate matter that is oily, photochemical smog, wood smoke block Dense fog, high humidity reduce air flow.	Feasible	ISI approved
2.	NO_x	Colorimetric	0.01-1.5mg NO_2/ml with 59 ml absorbing reagent and rate of 200 ml/min. for 24hrs the range of this method is 20-74mg/m^3 NO_2	—	SO_2 interference eliminated by converting it to H_2SO_4 with H_2O_2 before analysis.	Feasible	ISI approved
3.	SO_2	Colorimetric (Sodium Tetra chloromercurate method).	Method applicable below 26 mg/m^3 if absorption efficiency of particular system is known (usually 0.35%). Beer's Law is followed through range of 0.1 to 1 OD units. (i.e. 0 to 35 mg in 25 mlrate. final solution.	Precision at 95% confidence level is 4.6 %	O_3 and NO_2 interference are removed by adding sulphuric acid. Heavy metal (especially Fe) interference is removed by adding Na salt of EDTA.	Feasible	ISI approved

Contd.

Table 2.1. Contd.

Sl. No.	Parameters	Method Chosen	Range & Sensitivity	Precision/Accuracy Stability	Interferences	Feasibility	Remark
4.	H_2S	Iodometric (Titration)	1ppm (or as little as 0.035 mg H_2S in 24 l of air can be determined)	—	Hydrogen selenide Hydrogen telluride interference, Carbon disulphide does not.	Feasible	ISI approved
5.	H_2SO_4 mist in air	Turbidimetric	lower limit is $O_3$1 mg/m³ (100mg/NM³) in 100 litre sample of air to 4mg/m³ (4000 mg/m³) or as low as 10mg in 10ml absorbing solution. Values exceeding 0.4mg in 100ml sampling solution may lose stability.	—	Coloured or suspended matter in large concentration will interfere. Silica in above 800mg/l of sample solution will interfere, Organic materials, sulphate salts.	Feasible	ISI approved
6.	Cl_2	Colorimetric	5-100mg/100ml of sampling solution (i.e. for 30 l air sample, range is 0.05 - 1 ppm) Increase of volume of air will extend range at lower end but within limits. Using Dilute sampling solution concentration of 1 mg/100 ml may be measured	26 chlorine concentration produced 26 times by two different methods were measured by this procedure with an average error of less than ± 5% of the amount present.	Free bromine, and magnanese (III, IV) in concentration of 0.1 ppm or above interfere. In solution, negative interference from SO_2 is significant, NO_2 interferes positively. Ozone may interfere positively.	Feasible	ISI approved

eter for which a calibration curve had already been prepared.

Estimation of Chlorine (Cl_2)

Sampling was performed by passing a measured volume of air through a fritted bubbler containing 35 ml of dilute methyl orange. Near a pH of 3.0, the colour of the solution ceased to vary with acidity. The dye was quantitatively bleached by free chlorine and the extent of bleaching was determined colorimetrically. A calibration curve with the blank was prepared earlier.

Estimation of Hydrogen Sulphide (H_2S)

Hydrogen sulphide in air was collected in a buffer containing 25 ml of cadmium sulphate solution at the rate of 1.5 litres per minute for 20 to 60 minutes. Hydrogen sulphide present in air produces a precipitate of cadmium sulphide at high concentrations. The gas, after acidification of the precipitate was determined iodometrically.

Estimation of Sulphuric Acid Mist in Air (H_2So_4)

Sulphuric acid mist in air was absorbed in 10 to 15 ml of water in an impinger. The sulphate in the sample solution was precipitated as barium sulphate and the turbidity of the suspension was measured spectrophotometrically. A calibration curve for the above process was prepared earlier.

Studies on the Water Environment

The basic approach to water quality characterisation studies is methodical planning and reconnaissance surveys of the area under study. The observations made during the course of these visits formed the substratum on which the entire methodology was based right from where, when, how much to sample down to how to analyse the samples.

The entire procedure of sampling site selection, sample collection, preservation and analytical techniques used for this quality characterisation studies are described below.

Selection of Sampling Stations

Sampling stations were selected depending on the following

criteria:

(i) Location

Water resources near industries and effluent channels were taken to find out the possible contamination due to the industry. On the same time, ground water near solid waste dumps were sampled to ascertain the extent of leaching.

(ii) Usage

Water, which is used to a large extent, is sampled to assess its quality. Discarded wells and hand-pumps were also tested to determine the cause for the degraded water quality.

(iii) Visual Observation

Obviously polluted, *viz* odoured / coloured surface water as well as ground water bodies were sampled for chemical analysis.

(iv) Distance from the Coast

Distance from the sea was used as a reference point to assess the extent of salt water intrusion.

Based on the above criteria, thirteen representative sampling locations were selected in the study area (Figure 8). One control location was also selected. This was at Bahour (a nearby village to the study area and identical in its setting to the study area but free from the impact of industrial pollution). The land-use map also proved to be very useful for this. Samples were collected from these sites during April, May, June, October '94 and January '95 and analysed for the various characterisation tests. Overall some 830 analyses were performed on 60 samples.

Selection of Parameters

Parameters to be estimated were selected depending on the use to which the water body (from where the sample had been collected) was being put to. This was done based on the guidelines laid down in IS:2296. The parameters studied include pH, Electrical conductivity, suspended solids, total suspended solids, acidity, alkalinity, hardness, chloride, dissolved oxygen, biochemical oxygen demand, chemical oxygen demand, sulphates, nitrogen, cadmium, mercury, iron, zinc and manganese.

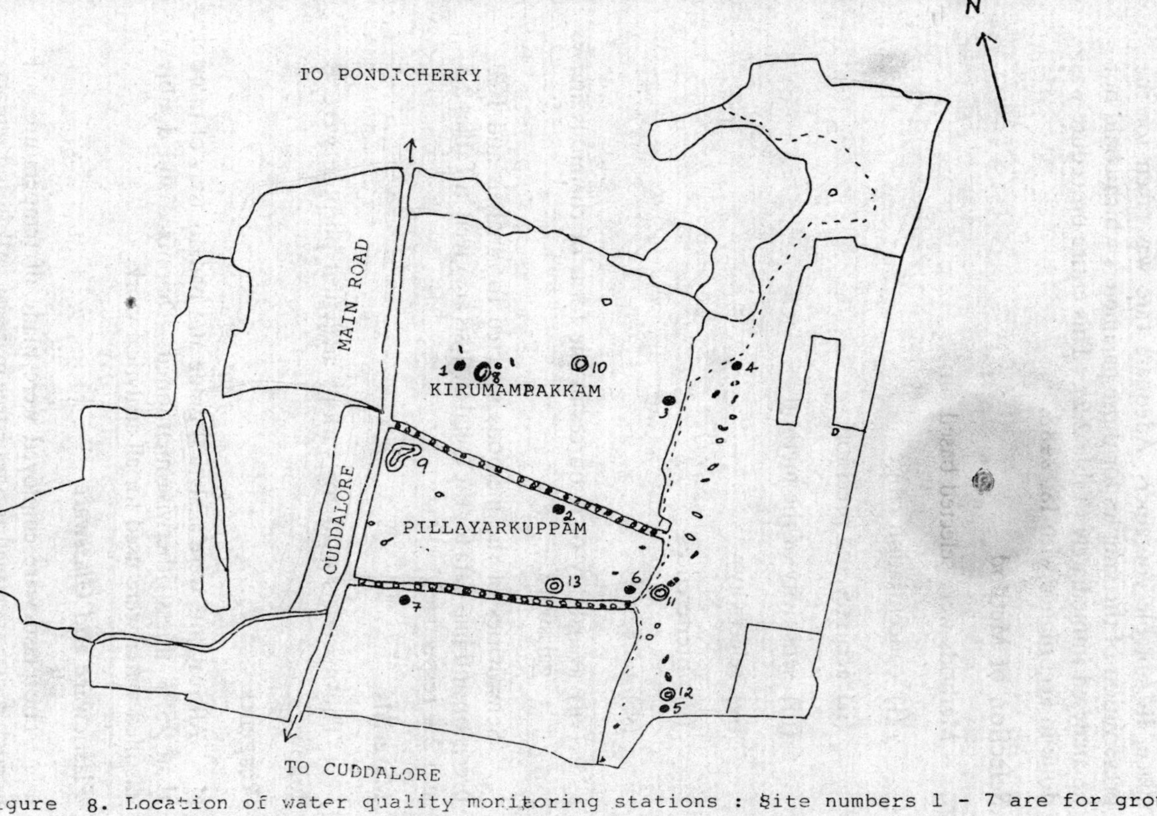

Figure 8. Location of water quality monitoring stations : Site numbers 1 - 7 are for ground water and site numbers 8 - 13 for surface water

Sampling and Preservation

Grab samples were collected from the selected sampling stations so as to ensure representativeness of the sample in time and space, in suitable containers. Adequate care was taken for the preservation of the samples for those parameters which could not be analysed immediately (Table 2.2). This entire procedure was done in accordance with IS: 2488.

Selection of Method

Methods were selected based on:

(i) concentration range

(ii) accuracy and precision

(iii) sensitivity of the method

(iv) selectivity

(v) interferences

(vi) time and

(vii) availability of resources in the form of chemicals and galssware.

Sensitivities of the methods selected for analysis and ICP precision and bias data for the metal analysis are given in Tables 2.3 and 2.4 respectively.

Materials

The materials used for various analytical purpose were as follows.

Reagents

All reagents were analytical grade and had an assay of more than 95 % unless otherwise mentioned. Deionized and doubly distilled water were used for all analytical work.

Plasticware and Glassware

The plasticware employed were made of temperature and scratch resistant, as well as odour-free material. Alkali and temper-

Table 2.2. Preservation Techniques for Water Samples

Sl. No.	*Parameter*	*Reco-mmended Sample volume*	*Type of Contai-ner*	*Preserva-tion*	*Allow-able holding periods*
1.	Acidity	100ml	P,G	4° C Refrigeration	24 hrs
2.	Alkalinity	100ml	P,G	4° Refrigeration	24 hrs
3.	BOD	100ml	P,G	4° Refrigeration	6 hrs
4.	COD	50ml	P,G	2ml H_2SO_4 per litre	7 days
5.	Chloride	50ml	P,G	Not required	7 days
6.	DO:Winkler	300ml	G	Fix on site	6 hrs
7.	Hardness	100ml	P,G	4°C Refrigeration	7 days
8.	Kjeldhal Nitrogen	500ml	P,G	40mg $HgCl_2$/ Litre 4°C Refrigeration	unstable
9.	pH	100ml	P,G	Determine on site	
10.	Phosphorous	100ml	G	40mg $HgCl_2$ 1 - 4°C Refrigeration	7 days
11.	Electrical conductivity	100ml	P,G	4°C Refrigeration	24 hrs
12.	Solids (TS,TDS&TSS)	100ml	P,G	4°C Refrigeration	24 hrs
13.	Sulphate	50ml	P,G	4°C Refrigeration	7 days
14.	Heavy Metals	200ml	P,G	HNo_3 5ml/litre PH = 2	6 months

Where, P = Plastic; G = Glass

Table 2.3. Sensitivities of Methods Selected for Analysis

Sl. No.	*Parameter*	*Method Used*	*Relative Standard Deviation*	*Relative Error (Percentage)*
1.	pH	Electrometric	—	—
2.	EC	Laboratory	—	—
3.	Acidity	Titration	1.8 $mgCaCO_3/l$	—
4.	Alkalinity	Titration	1.0 $mgCaCO_3/l$	—
5.	Chloride	Argentometric	4.2%	1.7%
6.	Hardness	EDTA-Titrimetric	2.9%	0.8%
7.	Salinity	—	—	—
8.	Phosphorous	Stannous Chloride	7.6%	4.3%
9.	Nitrogen	Macro-Kjeldahl	104%	70%
10.	Dissolved Oxygen	Azide Modification Iodometric	60 mg/l	—
11.	BOD	5 day test	—	—
12.	COD	Closed Reflux	±13mg/l	—
13.	Sulphate	Turbidimetric	0.13mg/l	—
14.	Heavy Metals	Inductively coupled Plasma Technique	—	—

ature-resistant Corning and Borosil glassware were used for estimation purposes.

Equipment

The following equipment were used for all the analytical work.

(i) Anamed make—top pan electronic balance model M 7000, capacity 100 gm, sensitivity 0.001mg.

(ii) Heating mantle—Concord Indian make with one litre capacity.

Table 2.4 : ICP Precision and Bias Data

Element	*Concentration ug/l*	*Total Digestion* ug/l*	*Recoverable Digestion* ug/l*
Arsenic	69–1887	X =1.0437 C - 12.2	X =1.0175 C + 3.9
		S =0.1239 X + 2.4	S =0.1288 X + 6.1
		SR=0.0874 X + 6.4	SR=0.0643 X + 10.3
Cadmium	17–47170	X =0.9182 C - 2.6	X =0.9658 C + 0.8
		S =0.1228 X + 10.1	S =0.0917 X + 6.9
		SR=0.0189 X + 3.7	SR=0.0327 X + 10.1
Mercury	13–1406	X =0.9544 C + 3.1	X =1.0049 C - 1.2
		S =0.0499 X + 4.4	S =0.0698 X + 2.8
		SR=0.0009 X + 7.9	SR=0.0571 X + 1.0
Iron	13–9359	X =0.8829 C + 7.9	X =0.9830 C + 5.7
		S =0.0683 X + 11.5	S =0.1024 X + 13.0
		SR=-0.0046 X + 10.0	SR=0.0790 X + 11.5
Maganese	42–4717	X =0.9699 C - 2.2	X =1.0056 C + 4.1
		S =0.0558 X + 7.0	S =0.0799 X + 4.6
		SR=0.0353 X + 3.6	SR=0.0448 X + 3.5
Nickel	17–47170	X =0.9508 C + 0.4	X =0.9869 C + 1.5
		S =0.0604 X + 4.4	S =0.0526 X + 5.5
		SR=0.0425 X + 3.6	SR=0.0393 X + 2.2
Zinc	7–7076	X =0.9356 C - 0.30	X =0.9500 C + 1.22
		S =0.0914 X + 3.75	S =0.0597 X + 6.50
		SR=-0.0130 X + 10.07	SR=0.0153 X + 7.78

* X = mean recovery, mg/l
C = true value, mg/l
S = multi-laboratory standard deviation, mg/l
SR = Single - analyst standard deviation, mg/l

(iii) pH meter - systronic model 335

(iv) Conductivity meter - systronic model 305

(v) Magnetic stirrer - Remi 2 MLH

(vi) Oven - Hemco Indian make with 30°C - 250°C.

(vii) Spectrophotometer - systronic make - model No.106

(viii) Gambaks BOD incubator - Indian make with temperature controller 0 - 50°C ± 1°C.

(ix) APR 3410 ICP with Minitorch

Specifications

Resolution	: First order 0.013 nm
Sensitivity	: pp_b levels
Spectral Range	: 189- 800 nm
Precision	: Relative standard Deviation 2%
Calibration accuracy	: ± 0.25 ppm
Gas purity	: 99.9% Argon gas
Flame Temperature	: 11,000 K
RF Generator	: 27.12 MHZ, 750 Watts output
Uptake rate	: 2-4 ml sample/min.
Spray chamber	: Conical 45 cc all glass demountable impact sphere.
Computer	: IBM S/2 Model 30
	Software PC-DOS V-3.0
	EPIC (Evolutionary programme for Instrument Control).Self guiding and operator interactive.

Analytical Methods

For this study, too, the most advanced methods were utilized. The bulk parameters were analyzed following the latest and internationally accepted techniques (APHA, 1992; Abbasi, 1995). The metal contents of the samples were analyzed by the state-of-the art technique of Inductively Coupled Plasma Atomic Emission Spectrometry in collaboration with IIT, Madras, India. The final concentrations were compared with the permissible/tolerable limits laid down by BIS (Bureau of Indian Standards - formerly Indian Standards Institute) (IS: 10500, 1993; IS: 2490, 1981) for different types of water usage.

Estimation of pH

pH was estimated potentiometrically using a pH meter involving a glass electrode and a reference calomel electrode. The lower portion of the glass electrode was dipped into the sample creating an electromotive force. The reference electrode was coupled with the glass electrode and the difference in e.m.f. was measured by the pH meter. Since pH depends greatly on temperature, temperature compensation was done during calibrating the pH meter.

Estimation of Electrical Conductivity (EC)

EC was measured using a conductivity meter equiped with a dip-type conductivity cell and resistance measuring device (essentially a wheatstone bridge). Since, temperature plays an important role in conductometry, temperature compensation was done during calibrating the conductivity meter.

Estimation of Suspended Solids

This was estimated gravimetrically. A well mixed sample was filtered through a previously weighed standard glass fibre filter paper and the residue retained on the filter paper was dried to a constant weight of 103°C - 105°C. The increase in weight of the filter paper represented the total suspended solids.

Care was taken to exclude large sample sizes to prevent formation of water - entrapping crust on the filter paper due to excessive residue.

Estimation of Total Dissolved Solids

This too was estimated gravimetrically. A well mixed sample was filtered through a standard glass fibre filter paper and the filtrate was evaporated to dryness in a pre-weighed porceilin dish and dried to constant weight at 180°C. The increase in dish weight represented the total dissolved solids.

Care was taken to exclude large sample sizes to prevent formation of water - entrapping crust on the filter paper due to excessive residue.

Estimation of Acidity

This was estimated by volumetric method using acid - base titration, where the sample was titrated against a strong base, generally, sodium hydroxide (NaOH). The amount of base used to raise the pH of the sample to designated levels was taken as a measure of acidity of the sample.

Indicator titrations with coloured or turbid samples was avoided. On such cases, acidity was estimated potentiometrically.

Estimation of Alkalinity

This was estimated by volumetric method using acid-base titration, where the sample was titrated against a strong mineral acid, generally hydrochloric acid (Hcl). The amount of acid used to raise the pH of the sample to designated levels, was taken as a measure of alkalinity of the sample.

Indicator titrations with coloured or turbid samples was avoided. In such cases, alkalinity was estimated potentiometrically.

Estimation of Hardness

Hardness was estimated by complexometric titration method, where the sample was titrated against di-sodium salt of EDTA with suitable metallochromic indicators like calmagite.

Heavy metal ions which interfere during hardness estimation was inhibited using sodiumsulphide (Na_2S). Organic matter interference was also removed by drying the sample and then heating in muffle furnace.

Estimation of Chloride (Cl^-)

Chloride was estimated through argentometric precipitation titration of neutral or sightly alkaline samples against standard silver nitrate solution. On highly coloured samples, where the endpoint could not be identified easily, aluminium hydroxide ($Al(OH_3)$) was added and this mixed solution was allowed to settle and then filtered. This filtrate was then used for further estimation.

Estimation of Dissolved Oxygen (DO)

DO was estimated by Winkler's iodometric method based upon redox reaction of manganese salt. It was reacted in the presence of oxygen with potassium iodide and the liberated iodine was titrated against standard sodium thio-sulphate ($Na_2 S_2 O_3$). In order to remove the effect of interfering materials, the azide modification of the Winkler's method was used.

Estimation of Biochemical Oxygen Demand (BOD)

The 5 Day BOD test consisted of filling with sample, to overflowing, an air-tight 300 ml BOD bottle and incubating it at 25°C for 5 days. The dissolved oxygen was measured initially and also after incubation. The BOD was computed from the difference between initial and final DO.

Estimation of Chemical Oxygen Demand (COD)

COD was estimated through dichromate closed reflux method. This was preferred over procedures using other oxidants because of superior oxidizing ability, applicability over a wide range of samples and ease of manipulation. The sample was refluxed in strong acid solution with a known excess of $K_2Cr_2O_7$. After digestion, the remaining unreduced $K_2Cr_2O_7$ was titrated with FAS to determine the amount of $K_2Cr_2O_7$ consumed and the COD was calculated in terms of oxygen equivalent.

Estimation of Sulphates (SO_4)

Sulphate in samples was estimated by turbidimetric method, where sulphate ion was precipitated in an acetic acid medium with barium chloride ($BaCl_2$) to form barium sulphate ($BaSo_4$) crystals. The light absorbance of the ($BaSo_4$) suspension was measured by a spectrophotometer at 420 nm and the sulphate ion concentration was then determined by comparing the reading with a standard curve.

Estimation of Nitrogen (Total Kjeldahl–N)

Organic nitrogen was estimated by macro-Kjeldahl method. Amino-nitrogen, ammonia, ammonium nitrogen of many organic materials was converted to ammonium sulphate in the presence of H_2SO_4. $HgSO_4$ was then digested forming a mercury ammonium complex and then decomposed by $Na_2S_2O_3$. After decomposition the ammonia was distilled from an alkaline medium and absorbed in indicating boric acid, from where it was determined by titration with 0.02 N H_2SO_4.

Heavy Metal Analysis

Samples in which heavy metals were to be analysed were first subjected to preliminary digestion, with nitric acid. The digested sample is then used for heavy metal estimation by inductively coupled plasma method.

Correlation Co-efficient Analysis

Multivariate linear regression between various components of ground water and surface water were done by using computer software—Lotus 1-2-3.

Studies on Land Environment

Studies on the land environment to assess the impact on land-use, especially agriculture as well as the impact of solid waste dumps were done as follows :

The Impact on Land-use, Especially Agriculture

The impact on land-use especially on agriculture was studied by a visual survey of the agricultural fields and by interviewing a large number of farmers in Pillayarkuppam-Kirumampakkam area. The findings were compared with similar survey done in the control area (Bahour). This area is typically similar to the study area in their topography, soil type, climate and other environmental conditons but otherwise free from any industrial pollution. The following agricultural data for the past 10 years were collected.

i) land under cultivation of food-crops and non-food crops

ii) total area under irrigated non-food crops

iii) total fallow lands

iv) land under non-agricultural use

v) land available for miscellaneous trees.

These informations were collected from the Department of Agriculture, Government of Pondicherry, India.

Impact of Solid Waste Dumps

To assess the impact of solid wastes, samples were randomly collected from different dumping sites (Public Place) and their leachates were studied in detail. Short-term leachate (30 minutes after the waste was wetted with water) as well as long-term leachate (24 hours after wetting) were analyzed. The key indicative parameters pH, EC, hardness, alkalinity and toxic metals were estimated. These parameters were analyzed following the latest standard methods (APHA,1992), described in this chapter under water environment.

3 The Key Findings

Studies on Air Environment

The results of the study are presented in Tables 3.1–16. The summary of the results showing the percentage of samples polluted are presented in Tables 3.17–19 and Figure 1 which shows *all* (100%) of the samples taken in the sensitive area, during the day as well as night, in the three seasons of Winter, Summer and Monsoon were polluted. Even at PIPDIC where, it being an industrial estate, much more liberal standards of air quality are applicable than in residential or sensitive areas, as many as 86% and 50% of the day samples taken during March 1994 and January 1995 respectively and 100% and 60% of the night samples during March 1994 and June–October 1994 respectively were polluted. Even in the other months the percentage of polluted samples ranged from 10% to 40% during the day and 40% to 50% during the night.

At the sampling site *Residential I up to 80%* of the day samples and 100% of the night samples taken during February 1995 indicated air pollution. Even in other months the percentage of polluted samples ranged from 13% to 60% during the day and 40% to 86% during the night whereas at the Site *Residential II* upto 100% of the day and night samples taken during February 1994 indicated unacceptable air quality. In the same site 60% and 20% of the day samples and 80% and 60% of the night samples taken during March - April 1994 respectively were polluted. Even in the locale *Residential III* where sampling was done during October 1994 20% of

Table 3.1 : Ambient NO_x Concentrations in Primary School (Sensitive Area)

Sl. No.	Months Sampled	NO_x ($\mu g/Nm^3$) 1	2	3	4	5	6	7	8	9	10
					Concentrations During the Day						
1.	February 94	96.7	165.5	124.6	95.75	-	-	-	-	-	-
2.	March 94	165.5	187.5	115.85	117.90	109.05	-	-	-	-	-
3.	April 94	68.6	69.2	82.46	64.64	52.42	50.55	[illegible]4.52	99.43	-	-
4.	June 94	50.3	62.9	34.5	68.45	87.9	-	-	-	-	-
5.	October 94	45.9	76.8	84.5	58.6	79.7	-	-	-	-	-
6.	January 95	170.75	113.05	107.04	125.15	140.89	150.19	134.99	131.14	232.78	225.86
					Concentrations During the Night						
1.	February 94	105.98	168.9	120.5	115.96	-	-	-	-	-	-
2.	March 94	189.6	199.8	105.6	118.8	120.85	-	-	-	-	-
3.	April 94	76.8	69.9	92.64	74.6	68.6	44.65	64.2	-	-	-
4.	June 94	56.9	83.1	38.9	56.5	67.8	-	-	-	-	-
5.	October 94	58.6	65.9	83.6	69.9	86.8	-	-	-	-	-
6.	January 95	199.65	163.09	106.06	135.62	142.98	148.69	129.99	136.64	250.98	230.69

Table 3.2 : Ambient SO_2 Concentrations in Primary School (Sensitive Area)

Sl. No.	Months Sampled	SO_2 ($\mu g/Nm^3$) 1	2	3	4	5	6	7	8	9	10
		Concentrations During the Day									
1.	February 94	9.58	10.12	15.65	17.85	-	-	-	-	-	-
2.	March 94	20.65	30.21	22.56	22.76	17.06	-	-	-	-	-
3.	April 94	18.0	22.6	29.4	20.56	16.85	22.36	18.98	99.43	-	-
4.	June 94	11.06	11.57	12.3	10.31	23.2	-	-	-	-	-
5.	October 94	15.08	16.78	11.8	9.9	21.8	-	-	-	-	-
6.	January 95	21.9	11.7	6.67	5.92	38.1	22.4	38.5	25.3	18.6	36.6
		Concentrations During the Night									
1.	February 94	28.69	15.38	26.95	16.95	-	-	-	-	-	-
2.	March 94	26.86	36.21	33.65	26.96	19.05	-	-	-	-	-
3.	April 94	20.0	21.08	34.6	28.65	13.95	21.63	28.98	-	-	-
4.	June 94	18.09	26.02	11.03	18.91	25.95	-	-	-	-	-
5.	October 94	22.1	26.86	13.08	12.06	22.1	-	-	-	-	-
6.	January 95	29.99	22.7	10.87	8.62	40.9	29.8	40.6	39.06	20.8	38.9

Table 3.3 : Ambient SPM Concentrations in Primary School (Sensitive Area)

Sl. No.	Months Sampled	SPM ($\mu g/Nm^3$) 1	2	3	4	5	6	7	8	9	10
	Concentrations During the Day										
1.	February 94	77.28	64.64	57.97	116.61	-	-	-	-	-	-
2.	March 94	105.76	119.71	64.23	75.63	62.68	-	-	-	-	-
3.	April 94	72.5	118.5	77.28	64.64	92.42	47.97	62.5	99.43	-	-
4.	June 94	57.42	74.07	27.15	71.79	80.4	-	-	-	-	-
5.	October 94	63.3	65.1	23.3	69.9	79.5	-	-	-	-	-
6.	January 95	232.4	57.5	202.77	60.01	113.8	95.46	110.29	78.5	80.2	93.4
	Concentrations During the Night										
1.	February 94	105.29	86.94	49.62	112.91	-	-	-	-	-	-
2.	March 94	106.8	126.97	86.23	73.62	59.69	-	-	-	-	-
3.	April 94	112.6	120.6	68.82	108.9	93.62	57.67	58.4	-	-	-
4.	June 94	68.62	73.08	28.62	79.29	101.2	-	-	-	-	-
5.	October 94	76.6	63.2	50.5	68.9	112.6	-	-	-	-	-
6.	January 95	236.5	158.6	199.6	65.02	108.9	100.6	111.3	65.8	79.5	96.5

Table 3.4 : Ambient Concentrations of NO_x in PIPDIC (Industrial Area)

Sl. No.	Months Sampled	NO_x ($\mu g/Nm^3$) 1	2	3	4	5	6	7	8	9	10
	Concentrations During the Day										
1.	March 94	145.83	133.41	187.5	165.65	204.55	96.4	89.4	-	-	-
2.	April 94	112.54	125.42	109.05	117.9	102.41	118.5	98.95	94.04	96.86	88.58
3.	June 94	64.76	82.5	133.65	125.67	111.49	-	-	-	-	-
4.	October 94	64.76	87.51	63.65	115.7	154.5	-	-	-	-	-
5.	January 95	200.48	194.12	190.93	78.01	75.83	81.44	163.65	82.5	64.7	154.5
	Concentrations During the night										
1.	March 94	155.9	183.42	190.6	180.75	195.65	105.7	150.9	-	-	-
2.	April 94	118.64	130.52	111.65	120.9	122.61	125.6	100.95	101.61	95.86	98.59
3.	June 94	75.86	62.5	153.65	123.68	121.69	-	-	-	-	-
4.	October 94	76.98	63.6	175.85	120.9	152.7	-	-	-	-	-
5.	January 95	208.48	196.12	202.6	98.06	65.93	89.56	199.65	89.5	55.7	166.7

Table 3.5 : Ambient Concentrations of SO_2 in PIPDIC (Industrial Area)

Sl. No.	Months Sampled	SO_2 ($\mu g/Nm^3$) 1	2	3	4	5	6	7	8	9	10
		Concentrations During the Day									
1.	March 94	101.39	218.16	38.03	102.58	65.68	126.5	108.4	-	-	-
2.	April 94	98.5	105.98	108.24	72.83	94.04	98.4	68.58	63.76	98.59	62.54
3.	June 94	26.33	12.08	20.55	25.7	35.6	-	-	-	-	-
4.	October 94	12.1	26.33	25.7	20.5	35.6	-	-	-	-	-
5.	January 95	24.55	11.24	22.77	35.5	20.5	12.1	26.3	35.8	42.3	18.9
		Concentrations During the Night									
1.	March 94	128.86	225.26	68.63	115.86	78.96	160.68	120.64	-	-	-
2.	April 94	108.6	110.69	119.6	121.2	100.9	99.6	79.08	56.65	78.6	63.64
3.	June 94	59.36	21.22	38.65	58.9	85.7	-	-	-	-	-
4.	October 94	21.2	36.84	29.8	30.65	45.8	-	-	-	-	-
5.	January 95	29.65	18.34	32.9	46.7	19.4	11.2	28.3	36.9	43.4	17.8

Table 3.6 : Ambient Concentrations of SPM in PIPDIC (Industrial Area)

Sl. No.	Months Sampled	SPM ($\mu g/Nm^3$) 1	2	3	4	5	6	7	8	9	10
	Concentrations During the Day										
1.	March 94	93.38	106.78	62.68	102.41	100.44	96.7	82.5	-	-	-
2.	April 94	116.58	64.09	122.63	98.58	92.34	89.4	95.96	82.07	90.05	88.5
3.	June 94	24.9	69.2	39.04	62.6	75.9	-	-	-	-	-
4.	October 94	28.2	65.7	40.0	63.7	81.2	-	-	-	-	-
5.	January 95	114.3	86.76	105.26	100.3	214.5	95.3	87.6	120.4	106.7	98.4
	Concentrations During the Night										
1.	March 94	92.29	105.98	75.69	105.41	99.33	106.7	92.6	-	-	-
2.	April 94	121.68	54.09	121.64	100.68	93.04	90.5	100.6	92.08	100.6	87.5
3.	June 94	26.8	65.3	35.05	65.7	76.8	-	-	-	-	-
4.	October 94	30.6	55.8	38.3	60.0	83.9	-	-	-	-	-
5.	January 95	118.9	89.67	120.27	98.4	213.5	93.4	67.8	119.4	99.8	67.4

Table 3.7 : Ambient NO_x Concentrations in Residential I

Sl. No.	Months Sampled	NO_x ($\mu g/Nm^3$) 1	2	3	4	5	6	7	8	9	10
		Concentrations During the Day									
1.	February 94	190.56	90.80	30.29	208.33	171.13	-	-	-	-	-
2.	March 94	95.5	126.56	68.63	149.42	72.12	65.66	79.45	-	-	-
3.	April 94	68.7	69.54	68.42	72.5	59.83	68.45	82.48	62.36	-	-
4.	June 94	30.47	32.5	48.94	42.02	89.15	-	-	-	-	-
5.	October 94	30.47	32.5	48.9	42.0	89.15	-	-	-	-	-
6.	January 95	170.1	74.49	69.83	134.8	115.25	112.78	102.21	79.9	80.5	73.65
		Concentrations During the Night									
1.	February 94	226.98	105.8	110.98	230.93	191.83	-	-	-	-	-
2.	March 94	115.6	130.85	79.93	160.82	99.98	86.76	80.96	-	-	-
3.	April 94	88.98	78.84	75.42	80.5	69.38	75.45	105.48	83.98	-	-
4.	June 94	50.87	82.6	88.64	72.20	99.51	-	-	-	-	-
5.	October 94	60.98	48.9	84.86	96.62	76.82	-	-	-	-	-
6.	January 95	198.6	94.50	86.93	156.98	120.25	116.98	99.21	69.8	96.5	65.7

Table 3.8 : Ambient SO_2 Concentrations in Residential I

Sl. No.	Months Sampled	SO_2 ($\mu g/Nm^3$) 1	2	3	4	5	6	7	8	9	10
		Concentrations During the Day									
1.	February 94	10.32	11.98	6.78	9.05	10.45	-	-	-	-	-
2.	March 94	28.66	40.01	36.49	32.55	29.6	25.66	39.45	6.48	-	-
3.	April 94	26.88	32.5	28.91	35.8	36.83	28.98	26.48	32.36	-	-
4.	June 94	4.9	6.7	5.5	9.4	16.4	-	-	-	-	-
5.	October 94	6.7	5.5	9.4	4.9	16.4	-	-	-	-	-
6.	January 95	3.13	13.38	3.04	6.52	4.92	8.30	7.51	9.2	10.3	8.9
		Concentrations During the Night									
1.	February 94	12.56	13.68	7.98	8.06	20.45	-	-	-	-	-
2.	March 94	36.66	45.06	35.69	38.85	36.66	45.68	38.65	-	-	-
3.	April 94	28.99	39.8	26.81	30.09	40.93	35.96	40.48	39.26	-	-
4.	June 94	8.6	9.9	5.8	10.6	20.9	-	-	-	-	-
5.	October 94	7.8	4.3	8.4	6.8	20.5	-	-	-	-	-
6.	January 95	6.83	20.98	5.08	5.62	8.85	10.50	9.81	15.20	12.98	9.80

Table 3.9 : Ambient SPM Concentrations in Residential I

Sl. No.	*Months Sampled*	*SPM (µg/Nm³)* 1	2	3	4	5	6	7	8	9	10
		Concentrations During the Day									
1.	February 94	130.05	130.00	95.96	82.07	61.86	-	-	-	-	-
2.	March 94	92.45	102.06	85.42	88.93	95.83	99.43	122.63	-	-	-
3.	April 94	62.68	75.41	68.26	89.45	96.75	72.42	67.09	99.43	-	-
4.	June 94	68.5	91.4	54.5	82.42	97.17	-	-	-	-	-
5.	October 94	72.69	100.5	72.8	96.85	105.36	-	-	-	-	-
6.	January 95	86.38	60.73	83.70	93.26	79.5	91.4	82.4	94.8	68.59	59.2
		Concentrations During the Night									
1.	February 94	129.65	150.66	100.86	80.96	98.6	-	-	-	-	-
2.	March 94	93.65	106.06	75.62	76.94	98.83	100.5	120.63	-	-	-
3.	April 94	65.68	50.41	65.26	92.45	98.57	60.62	65.09	98.75	-	-
4.	June 94	70.05	85.4	60.65	90.05	100.19	-	-	-	-	-
5.	October 94	65.9	89.9	65.9	80.5	96.3	-	-	-	-	-
6.	January 95	85.98	63.93	80.95	99.26	86.05	93.5	80.5	91.98	70.6	85.3

Table 3.10 : Ambient NO_x Concentrations in Residential II

Sl. No.	*Months Sampled*	NO_x ($\mu g/Nm^3$) 1	2	3	4	5	6	7	8	9	10
					Concentrations During the Day						
1.	February 94	208.00	123.29	212.3	124.77	135.39	117.42	-	-	-	-
2.	March 94	65.66	105.55	85.88	167.99	78.5	-	-	-	-	-
3.	April 94	75.5	58.86	62.35	82.56	56.84	-	-	-	-	-
					Concentrations During the Night						
1.	February 94	215.0	133.39	211.4	150.77	145.40	122.92	-	-	-	-
2.	March 94	82.96	120.65	95.99	156.96	72.6	-	-	-	-	-
3.	April 94	96.7	88.96	72.25	83.96	47.95	-	-	-	-	-

Table 3.11 : Ambient SO_2 Concentrations in Residential II

Sl. No.	Months Sampled	SO_2 ($\mu g/Nm^3$) 1	2	3	4	5	6	7	8	9	10
		Concentrations During the Day									
1.	February 94	15.55	12.32	20.6	12.72	13.39	17.23	-	-	-	-
2.	March 94	14.09	28.79	25.34	20.03	21.04	-	-	-	-	-
3.	April 94	46.5	38.51	32.68	28.91	28.56	-	-	-	-	-
		Concentrations During the Night									
1.	February 94	26.65	18.92	28.9	32.82	19.29	16.36	-	-	-	-
2.	March 94	34.29	26.68	33.34	19.09	22.05	-	-	-	-	-
3.	April 94	57.6	39.6	35.9	30.8	38.6	-	-	-	-	-

Table 3.12 : Ambient SPM Concentrations in Residential II

Sl.	*Months*	*SPM* ($\mu g/Nm^3$)									
No.	*Sampled*	*1*	*2*	*3*	*4*	*5*	*6*	*7*	*8*	*9*	*10*
		Concentrations During the Day									
1.	February 94	63.08	90.05	85.06	89.42	76.97	63.04	-	-	-	-
2.	March 94	96.75	95.83	67.09	72.42	68.4	-	-	-	-	-
3.	April 94	125.4	66.82	92.56	76.84	64.55	-	-	-	-	-
		Concentrations During the Night									
1.	February 94	65.86	89.12	83.71	90.63	86.98	65.65	-	-	-	-
2.	March 94	97.85	86.93	70.12	82.02	65.4	-	-	-	-	-
3.	April 94	130.5	56.92	95.65	75.83	63.55	-	-	-	-	-

Table 3.13 : Ambient NO_x Concentrations in Residential III

Sl. No.	Months Sampled	NO_x ($\mu g/Nm^3$) 1	2	3	4	5	6	7	8	9	10
		Concentrations During the Day									
1.	April 94	58.95	72.12	94.17	79.45	68.75	-	-	-	-	-
		Concentrations During the Night									
1.	April 94	65.65	82.38	100.78	80.25	70.65	-	-	-	-	-

Table 3.14 : Ambient SO_2 Concentrations in Residential III

Sl. No.	Months Sampled	SO_2 ($\mu g/Nm^3$) 1	2	3	4	5	6	7	8	9	10
		Concentrations During the Day									
1.	April 94	23.05	28.08	17.24	15.45	15.78	-	-	-	-	-
		Concentrations During the Night									
1.	April 94	50.12	29.09	20.30	20.67	18.98	-	-	-	-	-

Table 3.15 : Ambient SPM Concentrations in Residential III

Sl. No.	Months Sampled	SPM (μg/Nm³) 1	2	3	4	5	6	7	8	9	10
		Concentrations During the Day									
1.	April 94	97.98	37.88	115.67	99.43	65.45	-	-	-	-	-
		Concentrations During the Night									
1.	April 94	100.63	39.64	110.65	97.67	70.56	-	-	-	-	-

Table 3.16. Ambient concentration Of Cl_2, H_2S and H_2SO_4

Sl. No.	Parameter	Number of Samples	Maximum	Minimum	Maximum permissible Limit*
1.	Cl_2 (ppm)	66	0.289	0.03	1
2.	H_2S* (mg/Nm³)	55	2.531	0.258	10
3.	H_2SO_4 (mg/Nm³)	47	2.35	0.007	50

* Limit as per Ministry of Environment (MOEn) Standards

Table 3.17. Summary of the Findings of the Air Quality Surveys : February '94 - April '94

S.No.	Location	February'94				March'94				April'94			
		Sampling hours		Polluted samples		Sampling hours		Polluted samples		Sampling hours		Polluted samples	
		Day	Night	Day	Night	Day	Night	Day	Night	Day	Night	Day	Night
1.	Residential I	120 hrs	120 hrs	80%	100%	168 hrs	168 hrs	43%	86%	192 hrs	192 hrs	13%	50%
2.	Residential II	168 hrs	168 hrs	100%	100%	120 hrs	120 hrs	60%	80%	120 hrs	120 hrs	20%	60%
3.	Residential III	--	--	--	--	--	--	--	--	120 hrs	120 hrs	20%	60%
4.	Primary School	96 hrs	96 hrs	100%	100%	120 hrs	120 hrs	100%	100%	168 hrs	168 hrs	100%	100%
5.	PIPDIC	--	--	--	--	168 hrs	168 hrs	86%	100%	240 hrs	240 hrs	10%	40%

Table 3.18. Summary of the Fndings of the Air Quality Surveys: June '94, October '94 and January '95

S.No.	Location	June'94				October'94				January'95			
		Sampling hours		Polluted Samples		Sampling hours		Polluted Samples		Sampling hours		Polluted Samples	
		Day	Night	Day	Night	Day	Night	Day	Night	Day	Night	Day	Night
1.	Residential I	96 hrs	96 hrs	20%	60%	96 hrs	96 hrs	20%	40%	120 hrs	120 hrs	60%	80%
2.	Residential I	-	-	-	-	-	-	-	-	-	-	-	-
3.	Residential III	-	-	-	-	-	-	-	-	-	-	-	-
4.	Pry. School	96 hrs	96 hrs	100%	100%	96 hrs	96 hrs	100%	100%	120 hrs	120 hrs	100%	100%
5.	PIPDIC	96 hrs	96 hrs	40%	60%	96 hrs	96 hrs	40%	60%	120 hrs	120 hrs	50%	50%

Table 3.19. Overall Tally of Polluted Samples

Sl. No.	*Location*	*Overall*			
		Sampling Hours		*Polluted Samples*	
		Day	Night	Day	Night
1.	Residential I	792 hrs	792 hrs	40%	70%
2.	Residential II	408 hrs	408 hrs	63%	81%
3.	Residential III	120 hrs	120 hrs	20%	60%
4.	Primary School	696 hrs	696 hrs	100%	100%
5.	PIPDIC	720 hrs	720 hrs	43%	59%
	Grand Total	**2736 hrs**	**2736 hrs**	**59%**	**76%**

the day samples and 60% of the night samples were found polluted. In no locality less than 10% of the day samples and 40% of the night samples taken in any month were free from pollution. Percentage of samples crossing the permissible limit for various pollutants (both for day and night) at various sampling points are given in the Figures 2–6.

The pollution was more severe during the nights than during the days. This may be due to fact that the atmosphere is generally more stable during the night than during the day and radiation inversion causes pollutants to persist longer. The ambient temperature of the study area was slightly higher than in the control area (Figures 7-9) wheras the relative humidity is higher in the control area than in the study area (Figures 10–12).

The studies reveal that the air in the Pillayarkuppam-Kirumampakkam area is grossly polluted all through the year. The majority of samples indicate that the air is unclean and falls below the standards of air quality prescribed by regulatory agencies CPCB (Central Pollution Control Board).

The seriousness of the situation can be gauged from the fact that wheras *the norms set by CPCB require that not more than 5% of the samples taken over an annum should fall below the stipulated standards,* this limit is exceeded in *all* the months by 100% to 20,000% !

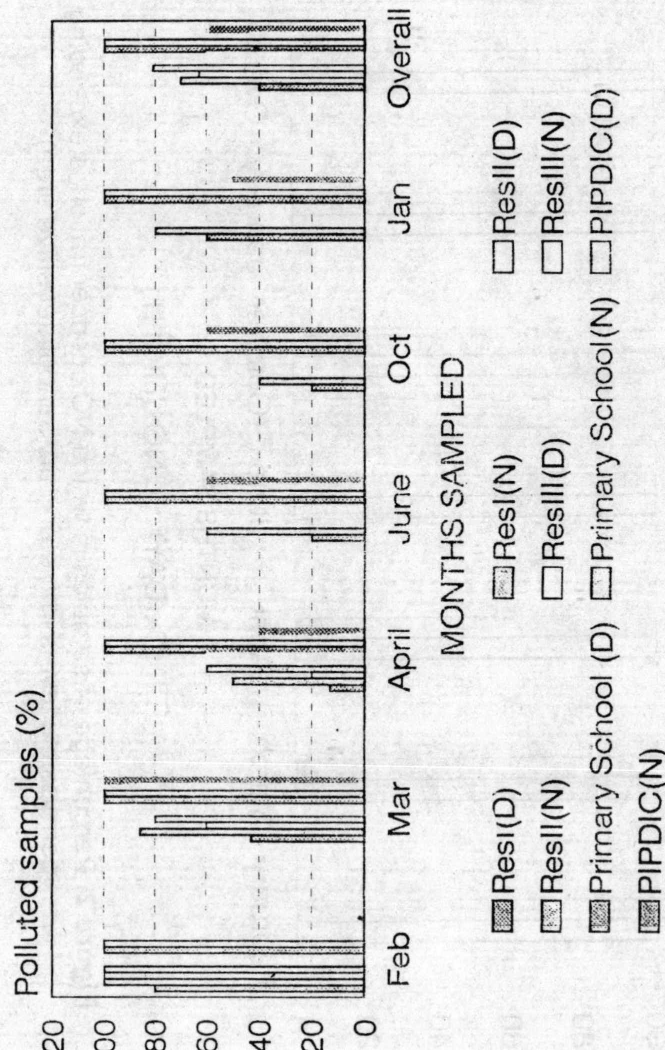

Figure 1. Extent of Air Pollution in the Pillayarkuppam - Kirumampakkam areas

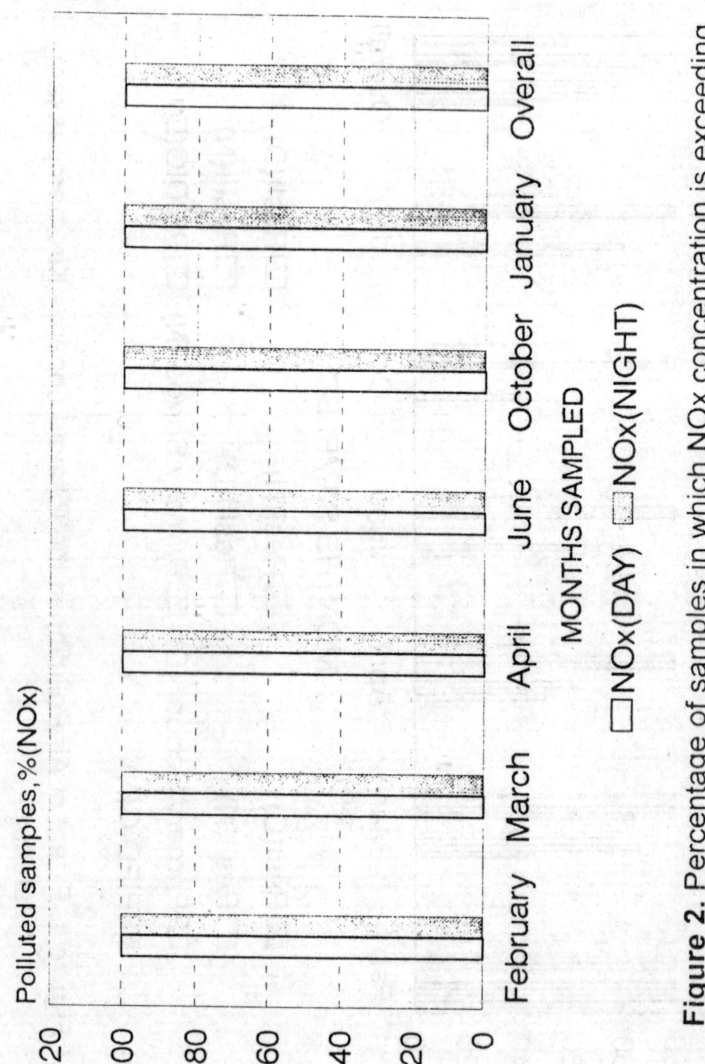

Figure 2. Percentage of samples in which NO_x concentration is exceeding permissible levels in the primary school(sensitive area)

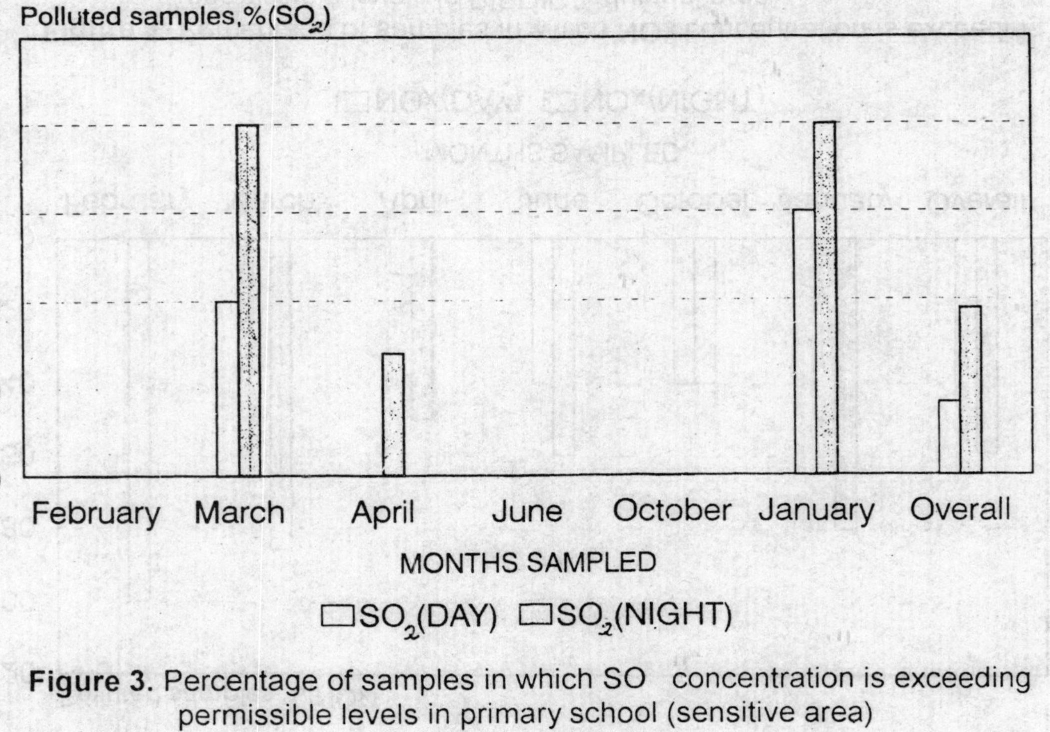

Figure 3. Percentage of samples in which SO concentration is exceeding permissible levels in primary school (sensitive area)

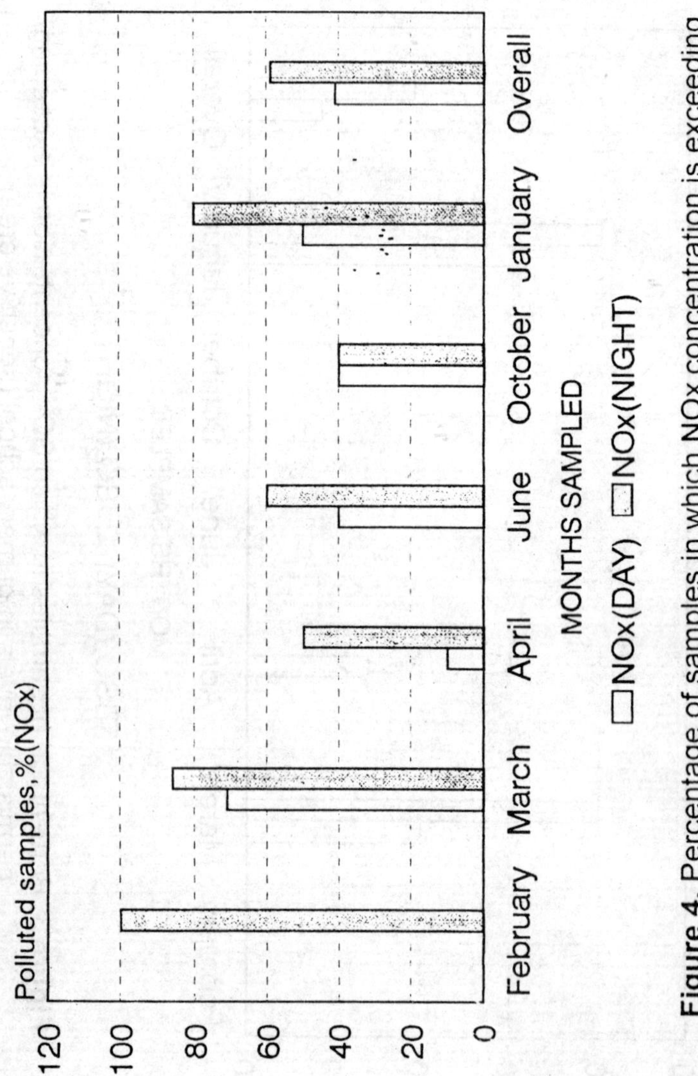

Figure 4. Percentage of samples in which NOx concentration is exceeding permissible levels in PIPDIC(industrial area)

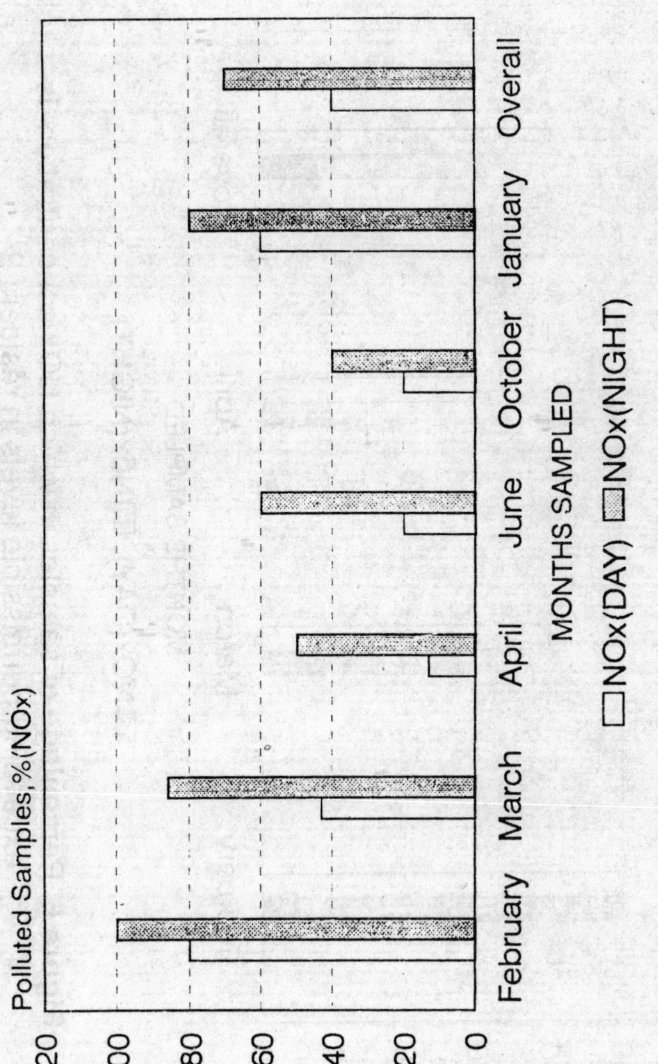

Figure 5. Percentage of samples in which NOx concentration is exceeding the permissible levels in resident 1

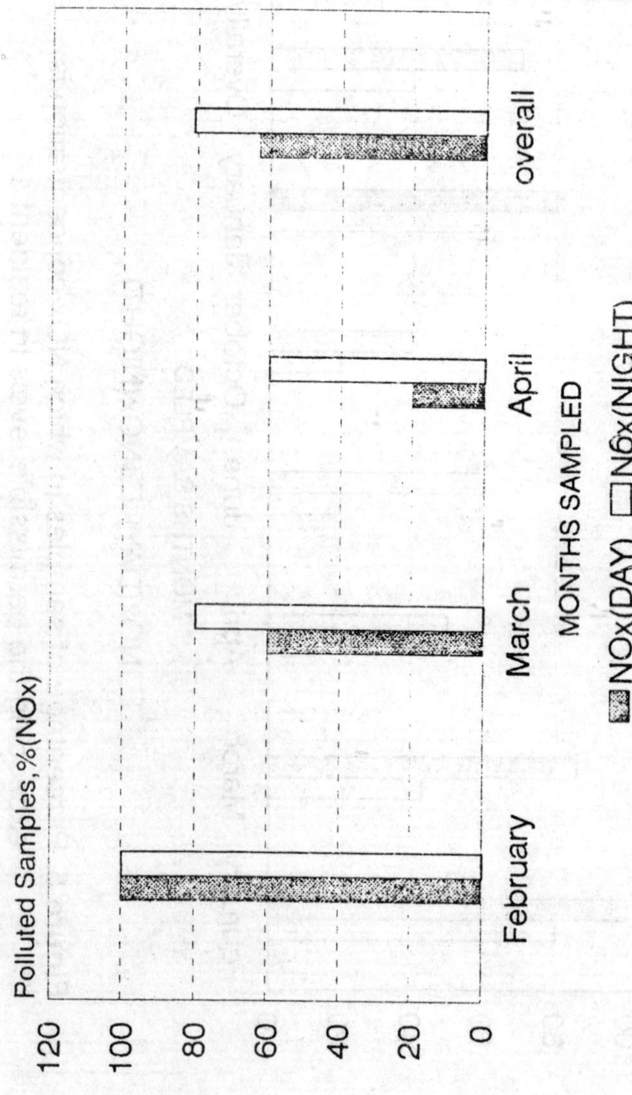

Figure 6. Percentage of samples in which NOx concentration is exceeding permissible levels in resident 2

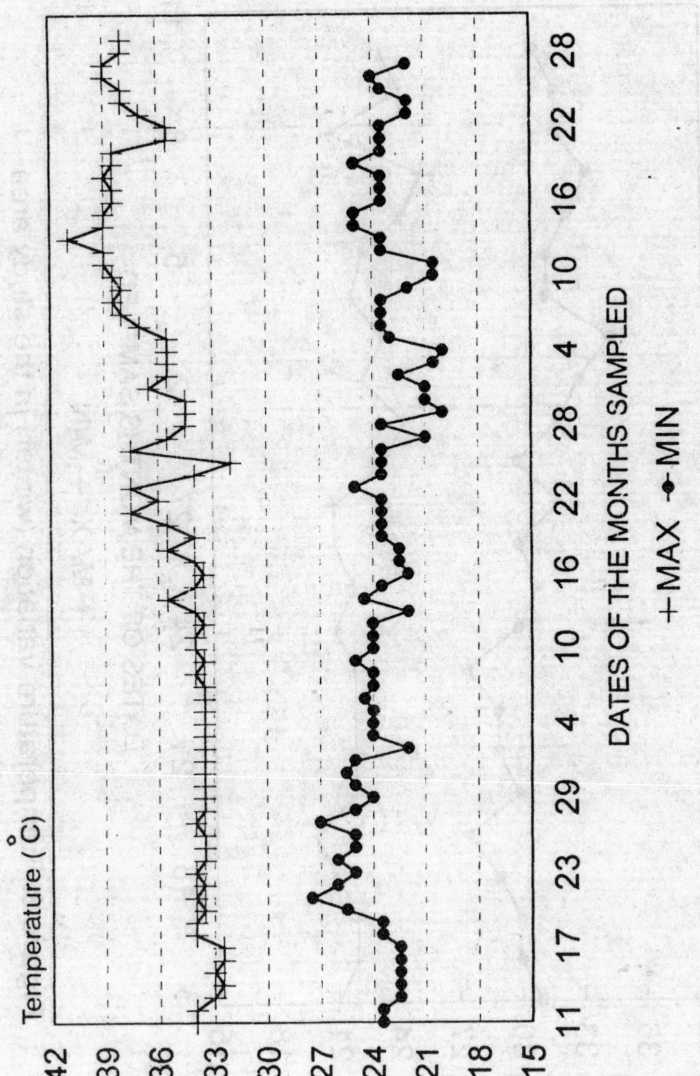

Figure 7. Temperature variation (summer) in the study area

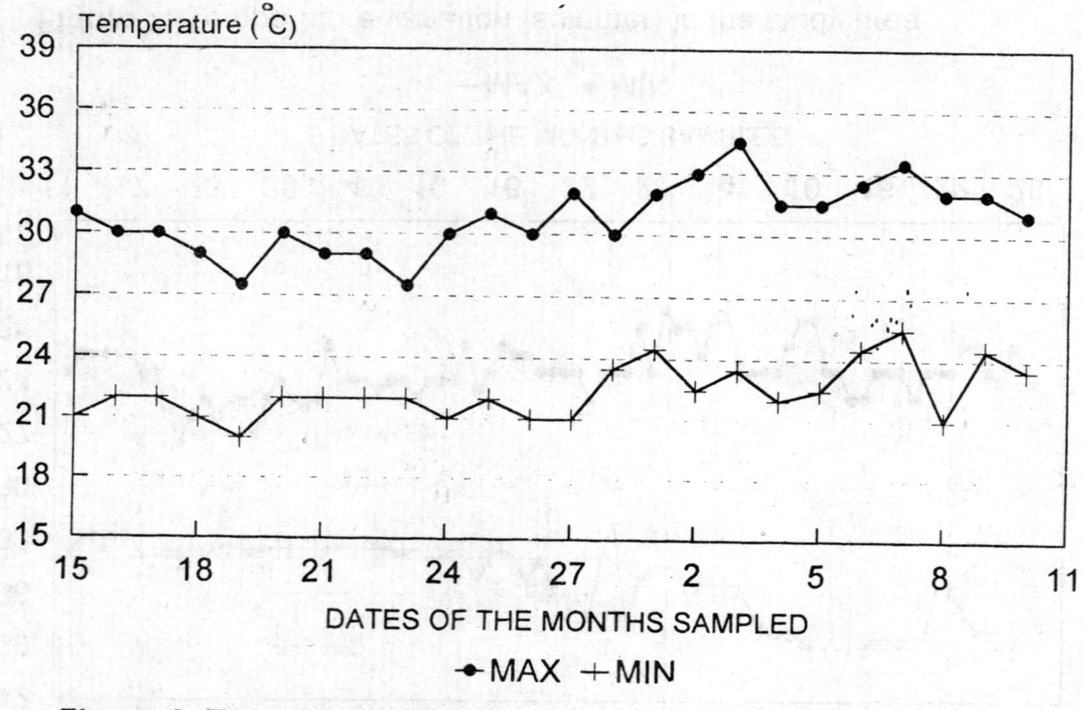

Figure 8. Temperature variation (winter) in the study area

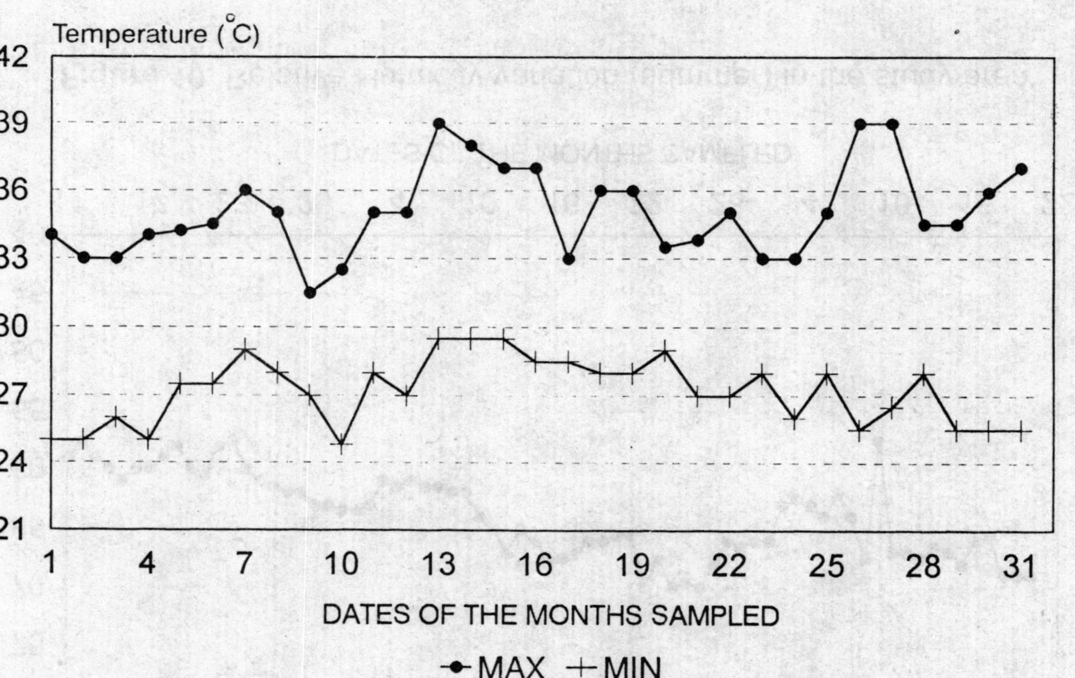

Figure 9. Temperature variation in the control area

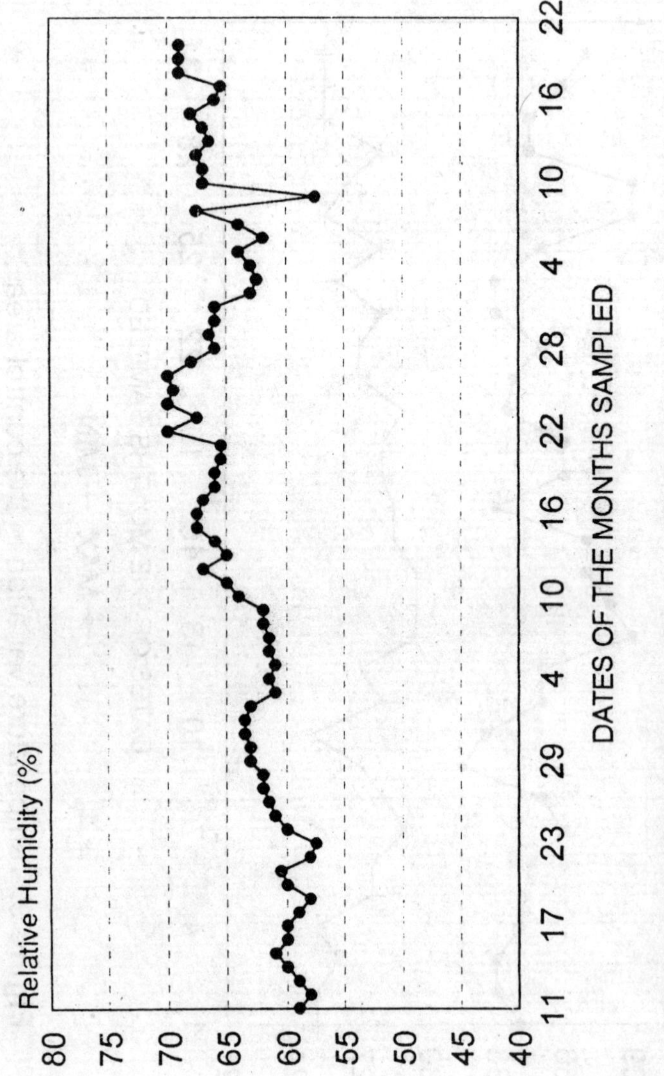

Figure 10. Relative Humidity variation (summer) in the study area

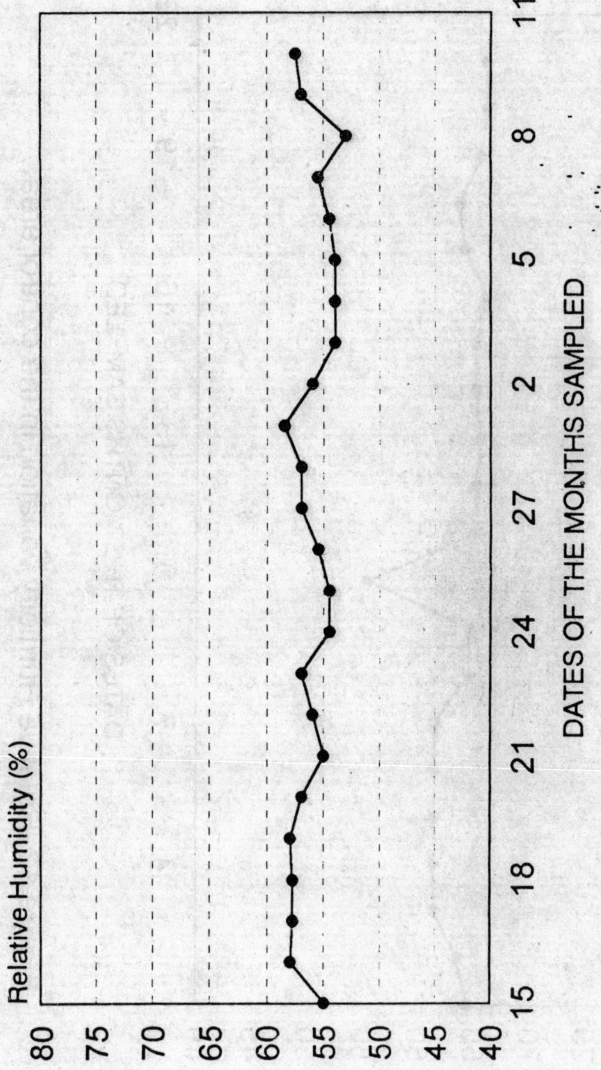

Figure 11. Relative Humidity variation (winter) in the study area

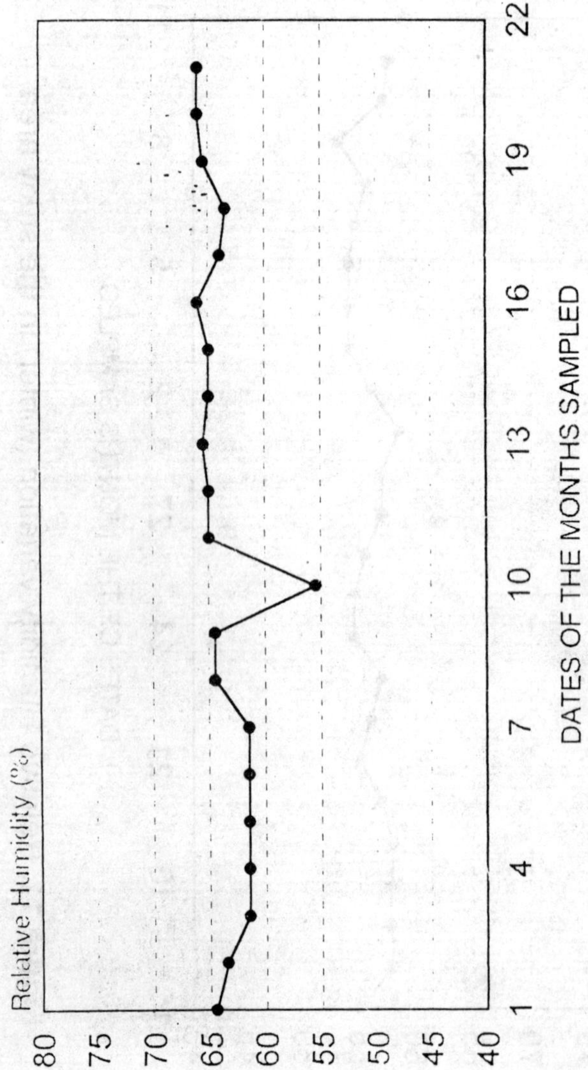

Figure 12. Relative Humidity variation in the control area

Thus none of the areas sampled in Pillayarkuppam-Kirumampakkam is free from air pollution and in some months, especially in the sensitive areas, the pollution is so damagingly persistant that the air is harmful most of the time. Further, in all cases, the norms of acceptable air quality as set by CPCB are violated.

Similar results have also been reported (Dandekar, 1989; Ravindra, 1991; Singh *et al*, 1994) in other typical industrial areas.

Important: All through the study, by a coincidence, the atmospheric stability was never at its worst possible. In situations - such as during heavy cloud cover - when the stability will be more than during the time of our studies, the concentrations of the air pollutants are *likely to be even higher and more persistant*, and their impact on the environment is *likely to be more severe.*

Studies on Water Environment

The analytical results of the water samples (Ground water/ Surface water) for various physical, chemical, and biological parameters are presented in the Tables 320–3.32 and Figures 13–23. The final concentrations were compared with the permissible/tolerable limits laid down by BIS (Bureau of Indian Standards—formerly Indian Standards Institute) for different types of water usage which is reproduced in Annexure II.

The results indicate that the water environment of the study area is also heavily polluted. It was observed that in *all* the samples the electrical conductivity exceeded the domestic water standards; in majority of cases doing so by several orders of magnitude (Figure 13). Other parameters also exceeded the limits, most of them doing so for *majority* of samples. The percentages of polluted samples for various parameters exceeding the limit for drinking water and domestic water are depicted in the Figures 24–37.

As mentioned above *all* the samples had electrical conductivity higher-than-permissible levels (Figure 24). These high values of EC are due to the high concentrations of ionic constituents present in the water bodies under study, and reflect the contributions from salinity intrusion as well as industrial effluents (Barbara & Harry, 1980).

Throughout the sampling period alkalinity was found to be

Table 3.20 : Concentration of various parameters in the ground-water samples of the sampling site 1 of the study area

S. No.	Parameter	April '94	May '94	June '94	Oct. '94	Jan. '95
1.	pH	7.5	7.5	7.6	6.5	--
2.	EC (μ mho/cm)	680.6	756.0	723.9	830.0	--
3.	TSS (mg/l)	0.1	0.1	0.1	20.0	--
4.	TDS (mg/l)	900.0	845.3	823.4	720.0	--
5.	Acidity (mg $CaCo_3$/l)	39.6	39.6	19.8	13.07	--
6.	Alkalinity (mg $CaCo_3$/l)	180.6	132.8	124.6	105.2	--
7.	Hardness (mg $CaCo_3$/l)	112.0	108.0	124.9	121.2	--
8.	Chloride (mg Cl/l)	32.5	32.0	30.5	22.9	--
9.	Salinity (mg NaCl/l)	53.2	52.8	51.3	49.2	--
10.	Nitrogen (Total) (mg/l)	1.6	2.4	2.1	2.4	--
11.	Phosphorous (mg PO_4/l)	0.1	0.1	0.1	0.03	--
12.	Sulphate (mg So_4/l)	257.2	219.1	192.8	185.12	--
13.	COD (mg/l)	2.8	1.7	0.4	2.9	--

Table 3.21. Concentration of various parameters in the ground-water samples of the sampling site 2 of the study area

S.No.	*Parameter*	*April '94*	*May '94*	*June '94*	*Oct. '94*	*Jan. '95*
1.	pH	8.0	8.1	8.0	7.6	7.6
2.	EC (μ mho/cm)	2135.0	1374.0	2492.0	2790.0	2580.0
3.	TSS (mg/l)	0.1	0.1	0.2	20.0	20.0
4.	TDS (mg/l)	1800.0	1600.0	1743.0	2660.0	2600.0
5.	Acidity (mg $CaCo_3$/l)	39.6	39.6	19.8	27.3	10.0
6.	Alkalinity (mg $CaCo_3$/l)	475.2	450.8	520.4	338.1	356.0
7.	Hardness (mg $CaCo_3$/l)	496.0	480.0	488.4	767.6	402.0
8.	Chloride (mg Cl/l)	353.0	329.6	304.5	412.97	281.27
9.	Salinity (mg NaCl/l)	582.4	543.4	500.3	681.4	464.09
10.	Nitrogen (Total) (mg/l)	1.4	2.6	2.3	2.6	5.6
11.	Phosphorous (mg PO_4/l)	2.3	1.6	0.3	2.6	2.9
12.	Sulphate (mg So_4/l)	1239.1	1092.7	1125.0	1056.3	1016.5
13.	COD (mg/l)	28.0	35.0	14.0	47.1	56.0

Table 3.22. Concentration of various parameters in the groundwater samples of the sampling site 3 of the study area

S.No.	Parameter	April '94	May '94	June '94	Oct. '94	Jan. '95
1.	pH	7.8	7.6	7.5	--	--
2.	EC (μ mho/cm)	1830.0	2394.0	2672.0	--	--
3.	TSS (mg/l)	0.2	0.4	0.4	--	--
4.	TDS (mg/l)	1150.0	1394.0	1592.0	--	--
5.	Acidity (mg $CaCo_3$/l)	39.6	19.8	39.6	--	--
6.	Alkalinity (mg $CaCo_3$/l)	178.2	297.0	330.4	--	--
7.	Hardness (mg $CaCo_3$/l)	404.0	397.0	384.5	--	--
8.	Chloride (mg Cl/l)	594.2	637.8	721.4	--	--
9.	Salinity (mg NaCl/l)	980.5	1052.4	1250.0	--	--
10.	Nitrogen (Total) (mg/l)	2.0	0.4	1.2	--	--
11.	Phosphorous (mg Po_4/l)	0.1	0.1	0.8	--	--
12.	Sulphate (mg So_4/l)	1550.1	1335.4	1241.3	--	--
13.	COD (mg/l)	6.0	4.0	10.1	--	--

Table 3.23. Concentration of various parameters in the ground-water samples of the sampling site 4 of the study area

S.No.	Parameter	April '94	May '94	June '94	Oct. '94	Jan. '95
1.	pH	7.5	7.2	7.7	7.3	7.8
2.	EC (μ mho/cm)	1694.0	3233.0	3492.0	1330.0	2660.0
3.	TSS (mg/l)	0.2	0.4	0.7	-	-
4.	TDS	1025.0	1234.0	1359.0	1260.0	1266.0
5.	Acidity (mg $CaCo_3$/l)	39.6	39.6	19.8	37.34	16.0
6.	Alkalinity (mg $CaCo_3$/l)	199.6	475.2	520.6	149.5	172.0
7.	Hardness (mg $CaCo_3$/l)	520.0	560.0	640.0	468.68	477.0
8.	Chloride (mg Cl/l)	752.9	763.7	770.8	718.47	656.65
9.	Salinity (mg NaCl/l)	1242.3	1620.2	1346.9	1330.47	1293.46
10.	Nitrogen (Total) (mg/l)	2.0	2.8	1.3	0.4	4.9
11.	Phosphorous (mg Po_4/l)	0.1	Negligible	0.1	0.026	0.1
12.	Sulphate (mg So_4/l)	1534.0	1294.4	1493.0	1206.18	918.67
13.	COD (mg/l)	4.0	8.2	9.3	4.3	7.2

Table 3.24 : Concentration of various parameters in the ground-water samples of the sampling site 5 of the study area

S.No.	Parameter	April '94	May '94	June '94	Oct. '94	Jan. '95
1.	pH	7.8	7.4	7.6	7.1	8.03
2.	EC (μ mho/cm)	1657.0	1041.0	1000.2	3000.0	1980.0
3.	TSS (mg/l)	0.1	0.1	0.1	-	-
4.	TDS (mg/l)	1980.0	2000.0	1894.2	1480.0	1420.0
5.	Acidity (mg $CaCo_3$/l)	39.6	19.8	19.6	11.20	18.0
6.	Alkalinity (mg $CaCo_3$/l)	237.6	200.5	241.4	326.6	190.0
7.	Hardness (mg $CaCo_3$/l)	324.0	300.0	351.2	517.17	302.0
8.	Chloride (mg Cl/l)	700.1	893.8	900.2	426.76	222.67
9.	Salinity (mg NaCl/l)	1155.2	1474.7	1743.9	1104.16	1367.4
10.	Nitrogen (Total) (mg/l)	0.8	0.9	1.0	1.6	0.83
11.	Phosphorous (mg Po_4/l)	4.5	5.9	5.9	2.2	2.6
12.	Sulphate (mg So_4/l)	1008.2	994.0	1023.4	1053.71	1097.81
13.	COD (mg/l)	53.0	60.0	49.0	33.33	80.0

Table 3.25 : Concentration of various parameters in the groundwater samples of the sampling site 6 of the study area

S.No.	*Parameter*	*April '94*	*May '94*	*June '94*	*Oct. '94*	*Jan. '95*
1.	pH	7.4	8.1	7.4	7.6	8.3
2.	EC (μ mho/cm)	2050.4	1976.0	2101.0	1200.0	1200.0
3.	TSS (mg/l)	0.1	0.1	0.1	--	--
4.	TDS (mg/l)	2200.0	2409.0	2743.5	1660.0	1720.0
5.	Acidity (mg $CaCo_3$/l)	19.8	Negligible	39.6	3.70	6.0
6.	Alkalinity (mg $CaCo_3$/l)	295.4	178.2	249.6	250.7	86.0
7.	Hardness (mg $CaCo_3$/l)	180.0	204.0	162.0	270.6	250.0
8.	Chloride (mg Cl/l)	120.5	142.0	152.0	187.0	128.9
9.	Salinity (mg NaCl/l)	198.8	234.2	265.0	308.6	212.7
10.	Nitrogen (Total) (mg/l)	0.9	2.8	1.9	2.1	0.83
11.	Phosphorous (mg Po_4/l)	0.1	Negligible	0.2	0.1	0.2
12.	Sulphate (mg So_4/l)	456.3	359.2	292.0	352.9	254.7
13.	COD (mg/l)	7.2	4.1	3.1	8.1	9.6

Table 3.26 : Concentration of various parameters in the groundwater samples of the sampling site 7 of the study area

S.No.	*Parameter*	*April '94*	*May '94*	*June '94*	*Oct. '94*	*Jan. '95*
1.	pH	7.9	7.3	8.0	7.1	8.2
2.	EC (μ mho/cm)	1586.0	972.0	828.0	1560.0	1500.0
3.	TSS (mg/l)	0.1	0.1	0.1	20.0	20.0
4.	TDS (mg/l)	3100.0	3000.0	2493.0	860.0	820.0
5.	Acidity (mg $CaCo_3$/l)	39.6	19.8	19.8	5.60	14.0
6.	Alkalinity (mg $CaCo_3$/l)	356.4	259.6	234.8	575.00	188.0
7.	Hardness (mg $CaCo_3$/l)	516.0	520.0	500.0	359.9	360.0
8.	Chloride (mg Cl/l)	352.7	358.6	368.0	138.9	146.5
9.	Salinity (mg NaCl/l)	581.2	591.7	629.5	229.2	241.7
10.	Nitrogen (Total mg/l)	0.8	1.9	2.3	2.8	0.46
11.	Phosphorous (mg Po_4/l)	0.8	0.9	0.2	0.06	0.04
12.	Sulphate (mg So_4/l)	1069.1	994.3	825.9	992.7	948.9
13.	COD (mg/l)	4.3	4.2	4.2	6.6	10.4

Table 3.27. Concentration of various parameters in the surface water samples of the sampling site 1 of the study area

S.No.	Parameter	April '94	May '94	June '94	Oct. '94	Jan. '95
1.	pH	8.5	8.3	8.7	8.03	8.00
2.	EC (µ mho/cm)	1594.7	1942.0	2012.1	1720.00	1650.00
3.	TSS (mg/l)	0.1	0.3	0.5	20.00	21.00
4.	TDS (mg/l)	1200.0	1231.0	1242.0	1020.00	999.00
5.	Acidity (mg $CaCo_3$/l)	19.8	39.6	39.6	11.50	9.50
6.	Alkalinity (mg $CaCo_3$/l)	300.5	386.8	317.2	363.40	370.50
7.	Hardness (mg $CaCo_3$/l)	388.0	360.0	372.0	281.80	290.00
8.	Chloride (mg Cl/l)	69.4	72.0	83.5	47.70	39.50
9.	Salinity (mg NaCl/l)	114.6	118.8	213.0	75.52	80.60
10.	Nitrogen (Total) (mg/l)	13.2	12.9	16.5	27.00	20.00
11.	Phosphorous (mg Po_4/l)	0.9	0.7	0.9	0.30	0.30
12.	Sulphate (mg So_4/l)	952.3	980.0	985.6	916.00	899.00
13.	DO (mg/l)	6.8	6.4	6.6	6.00	5.50
14.	BOD (mg/l)	0.3	0.4	0.5	1.40	2.00
15.	COD (mg/l)	6.0	6.0	7.2	7.90	8.00

Table 3.28 : Concentration of various parameters in the surface water samples of the sampling site 2 of the study area

S.No.	Parameter	April '94	May '94	June '94	Oct. '94	Jan. '9
1.	pH	8.3	8.00	8.1	8.4	8.5
2.	EC (μ mho/cm)	1420.0	1426.00	1452.00	3060.0	1620.0
3.	TSS (mg/l)	0.1	0.30	0.3	80.0	80.0
4.	TDS (mg/l)	1750.0	1724.00	1777.0	1440.0	1840.0
5.	Acidity (mg $CaCo_3$/l)	Negligible	19.80	39.6	Negligible	4.0
6.	Alkalinity (mg $CaCo_3$/l)	252.0	240.00	162.00	409.40	110.0
7.	Hardness (mg $CaCo_3$/l)	252.0	242.00	263.0	335.3	271.0
8.	Chloride (mg Cl/l)	300.7	313.90	371.9	581.5	242.2
9.	Salinity (mg NaCl/l)	496.1	518.00	529.3	959.5	399.60
10.	Nitrogen (Total mg /l)	27.2	28.50	33.4	33.7	0.7
11.	Phosphorous (mg P/l)	Negligible	0.02	0.04	0.90	0.80
12.	Sulphate (mg So_4/l)	693.6	488.10	642.3	440.6	730.8
13.	DO (mg/l)	6.0	8.20	7.5	6.0	7.6
14.	BOD (mg/l)	4.5	3.90	6.2	4.0	5.5
15.	COD (mg/l)	46.0	38.00	52.1	29.0	41.0

Table 3.29 : Concentration of various parameters in the surface water samples of the sampling site 3 of the study area

S.No.	*Parameter*	*April '94*	*May '94*	*June '94*	*Oct. '94*	*Jan. '9*
1.	pH	8.4	8.5	8.30	--	7.90
2.	EC (μ mho/cm)	3111.0	1998.0	3245.00	--	2280.00
3.	TSS (mg/l)	0.1	0.3	0.40	--	80.00
4.	TDS (mg/l)	1640.0	1648.0	1723.00	--	3560.00
5.	Acidity (mg $CaCo_3$/l)	39.6	19.8	39.60	--	10.80
6.	Alkalinity (mg $CaCo_3$/l)	328.0	316.0	348.00	--	240.00
7.	Hardness (mg $CaCo_3$/l)	350.0	316.0	362.00	--	400.00
8.	Chloride (mg Cl/l)	752.6	825.7	932.70	--	682.04
9.	Salinity (mg NaCl/l)	1241.8	1362.5	1429.40	--	1135.36
10.	Nitrogen (Total) (mg/l)	2.0	3.4	3.00	--	24.20
11.	Phosphorous (mg Po_4/l)	1.6	0.7	1.30	--	2.01
12.	Sulphate (mg So_4/l)	1316.4	860.6	1042.00	--	428.80
13.	DO (mg/l)	4.9	6.3	5.50	--	3.00
14.	BOD (mg/l)	4.5	3.2	4.00	--	4.50
15.	COD (mg/l)	60.0	58.0	67.50	---	76.00

Table 3.30 : Concentration of various parameters in the surfacewater samples of the sampling site 4 of the study area

S.No.	*Parameter*	*April '94*	*May '94*	*June '94*	*Oct. '94*	*Jan. '95*
1.	pH	8.1	8.5	8.3	--	8.60
2.	EC (μ mho/cm)	3904.0	2401.0	2894.0	--	2700.00
3.	TSS (mg/l)	0.1	0.1	0.3	--	40.00
4.	TDS (mg/l)	3200.0	3644.0	4592.0	--	3520.00
5.	Acidity (mg $CaCo_3l$)	19.8	39.6	19.8	--	12.00
6.	Alkalinity (mg $CaCo_3/l$)	780.0	759.2	753.40	--	306.00
7.	Hardness (mg $CaCo_3/l$)	780.0	759.2	769.5	--	445.00
8.	Chloride (mg Cl/l)	946.4	1291.3	1523.7	--	1158.20
9.	Salinity (mg NaCl/l)	1561.6	2130.6	2792.3	--	1261.05
10.	Nitrogen (Total) (mg/l)	0.8	1.8	1.9	--	0.84
11.	Phosphorous (mg Po_4/l)	0.3	0.2	0.2	--	0.80
12.	Sulphate (mg So_4/l)	1227.3	1050.0	1239.6	--	828.20
13.	DO (mg/l)	0.9	0.4	0.3	--	0.80
14.	BOD (mg/l)	3.9	4.7	5.2	--	3.60
15.	COD (mg/l)	28.0	36.0	32.5	--	70.40

Table 3.31 : Concentration of various parameters in the surface water samples of the sampling site 5 of the study area

S.No.	Parameter	April '94	May '94	June '94	Oct. '94	Jan. '95
1.	pH	8.4	8.1	8.6	7.9	7.40
2.	EC (μ mho/cm)	3599.0	2239.0	3242.0	3090.0	3420.00
3.	TSS (mg/l)	0.1	0.1	0.1	20.0	40.00
4.	TDS (mg/l)	3100.0	3000.0	3200.0	1720.0	3960.00
5.	Acidity (mg $CaCo_3$/l)	39.6	19.8	39.6	18.67	14.00
6.	Alkalinity (mg $CaCo_3$/l)	828.0	827.6	835.90	319.7	122.00
7.	Hardness (mg $CaCo_3$/l)	816.0	820.0	842.0	585.8	700.00
8.	Chloride (mg Cl/l)	1025.4	1691.3	1842.7	637.1	650.40
9.	Salinity (mg NaCl/l)	1691.9	2790.6	3242.4	1051.1	1073.20
10.	Nitrogen (Total) (mg/l)	0.8	2.3	2.0	2.8	1.80
11.	Phosphorous (mg Po_4/l)	3.7	2.5	2.7	0.7	0.80
12.	Sulphate (mg So_4/l)	1115.5	1025.6	1297.4	928.3	1096.40
13.	DO	5.4	6.9	4.3	2.0	2.10
14.	BOD (mg/l)	0.3	1.3	4.4	1.8	3.30
15.	COD (mg/l)	10.0	9.3	8.5	9.4	8.20

Table 3.32 : Concentration of various parameters in the surface water samples of the sampling site 6 of the study area

S.No.	Parameter	April '94	May '94	June '94	Oct. '94	Jan. '95
1.	pH	8.8	7.9	8.30	8.40	8.06
2.	EC (μ mho/cm)	2684.0	2457.0	2993.80	5100.00	3180.00
3.	TSS (mg/l)	0.1	0.1	0.10	40.00	120.00
4.	TDS (mg/l)	2250.0	2150.0	2345.00	2260.00	4320.00
5.	Acidity (mg $CaCo_3$/l)	39.6	19.8	19.80	Nil	6.00
6.	Alkalinity (mg $CaCo_3$/l)	990.0	1089.0	1250.00	772.80	406.00
7.	Hardness (mg $CaCo_3$/l)	396.0	424.0	450.00	517.12	355.00
8.	Chloride (mg Cl/l)	753.4	705.8	802.90	620.80	376.90
9.	Salinity (mg NaCl/l)	1243.1	1152.5	1795.30	1024.40	622.02
10.	Nitrogen (Total) (mg/l)	34.7	52.5	49.90	52.30	0.650
11.	Phosphorous (mg Po_4/l)	0.8	0.8	0.80	0.90	0.60
12.	Sulphate (mg So_4/l)	82.7	60.5	72.40	96.50	50.50
13.	DO (mg/l)	1.1	0.9	0.40	1.50	1.30
14.	BOD (mg/l)	5.3	7.2	10.10	3.60	3.60
15.	COD (mg/l)	28.0	32.0	41.10	20.00	28.00

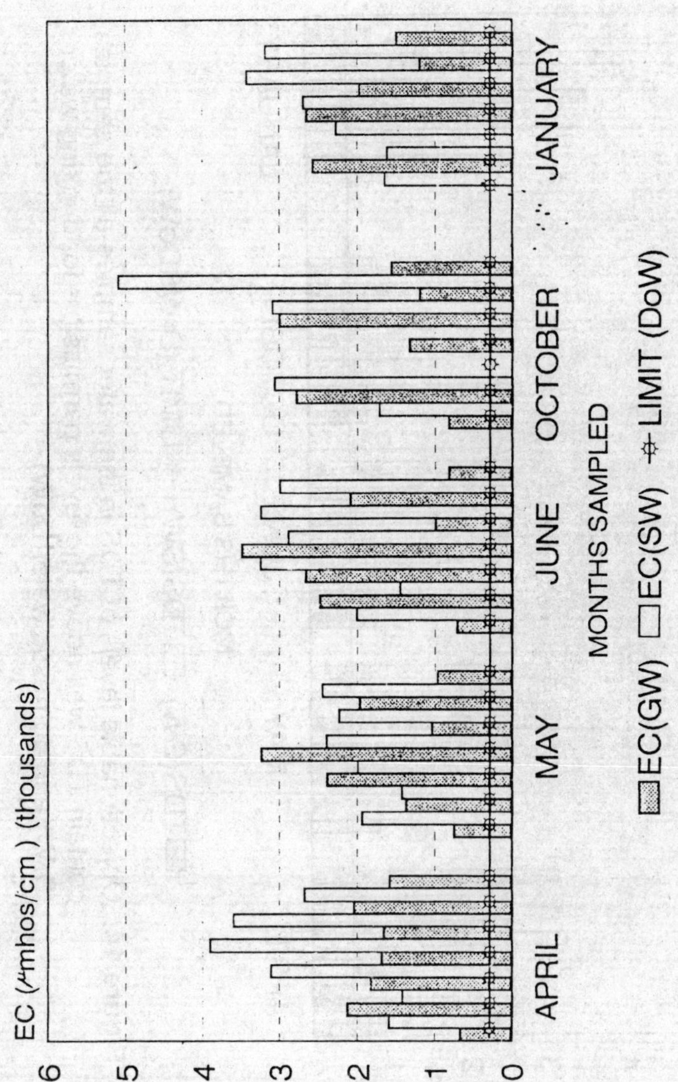

Figure 13. Excessive EC of the water samples

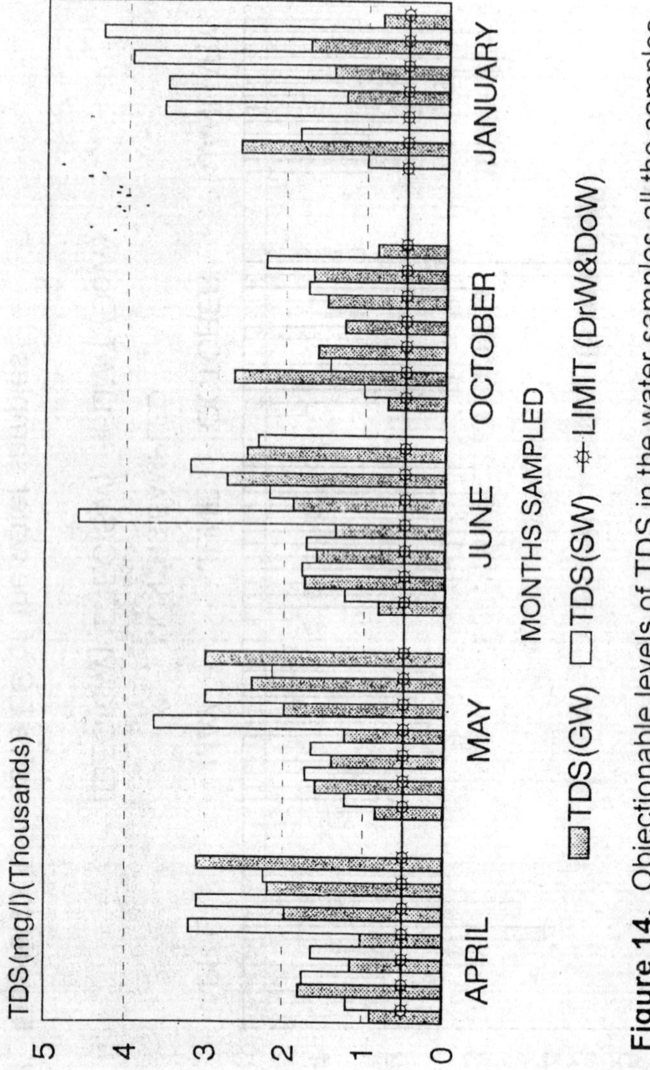

Figure 14. Objectionable levels of TDS in the water samples-all the samples contain TDS well above the levels permissible for drinking water (DrW) and domestic water(DoW)

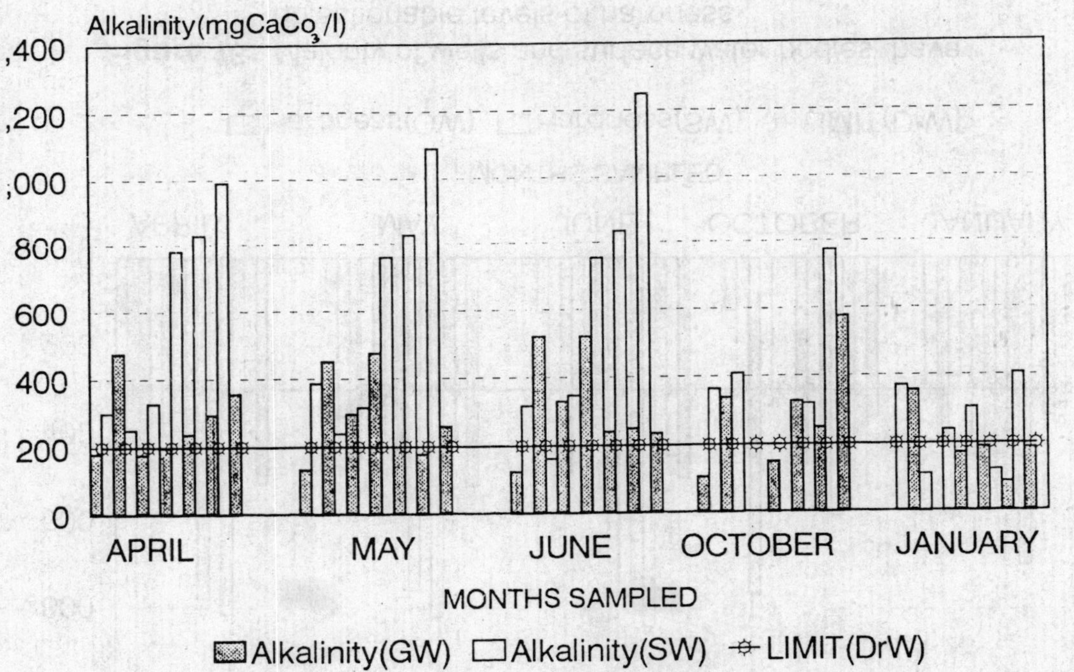

Figure 15. Excessive alkalinity levels in the majority of water samples

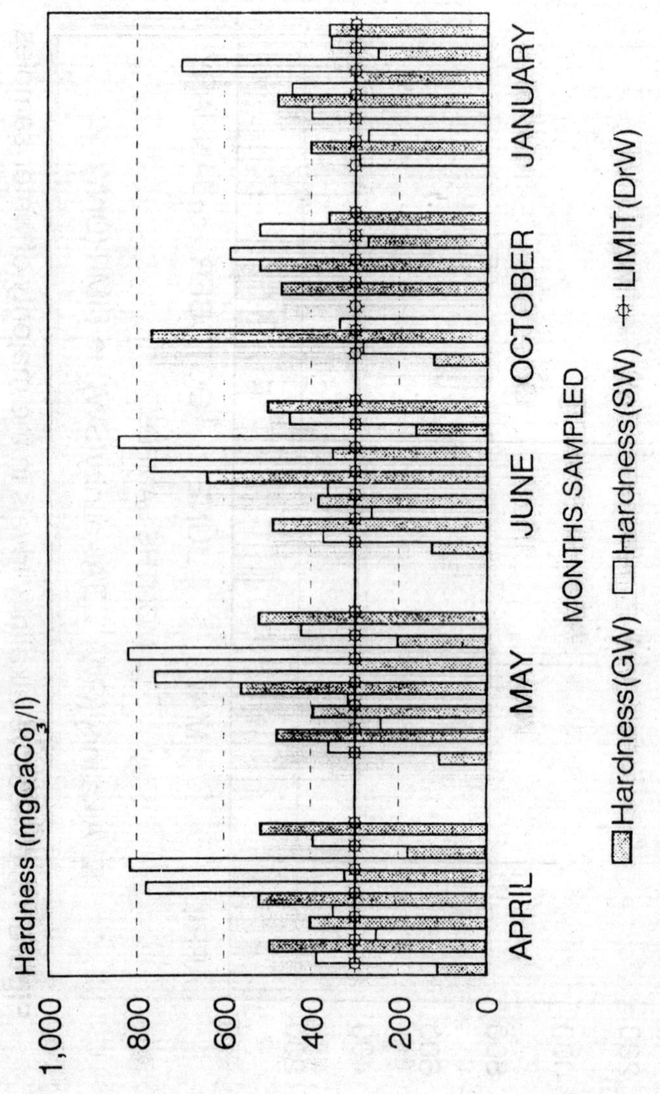

Figure 16. Majority of wells and surface water bodies have objectionable levels of hardness

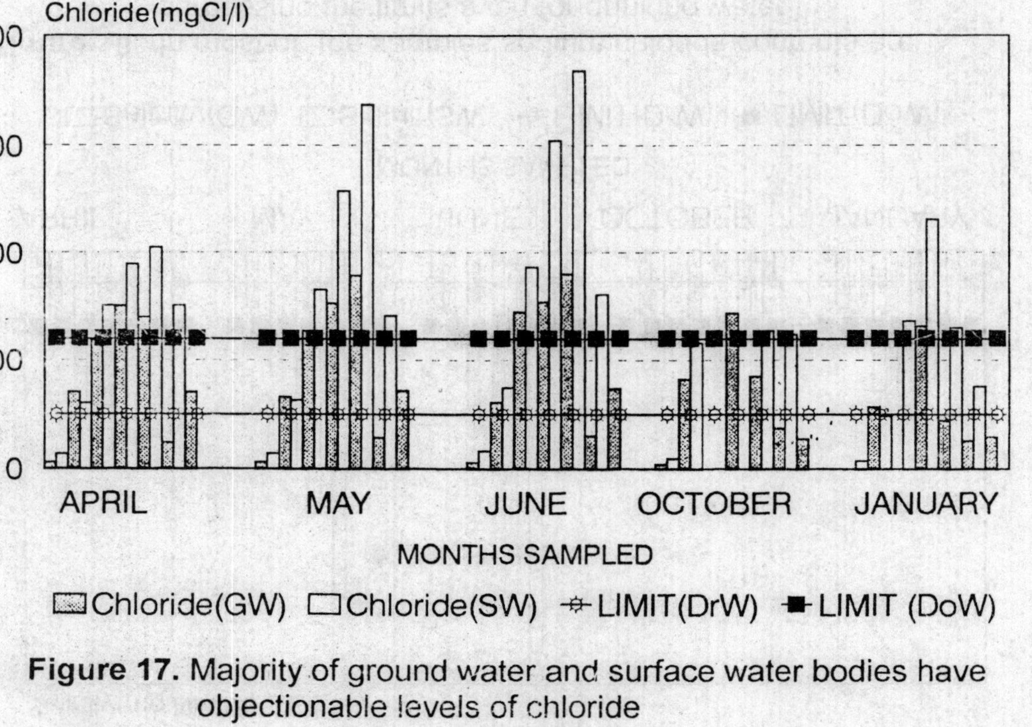

Figure 17. Majority of ground water and surface water bodies have objectionable levels of chloride

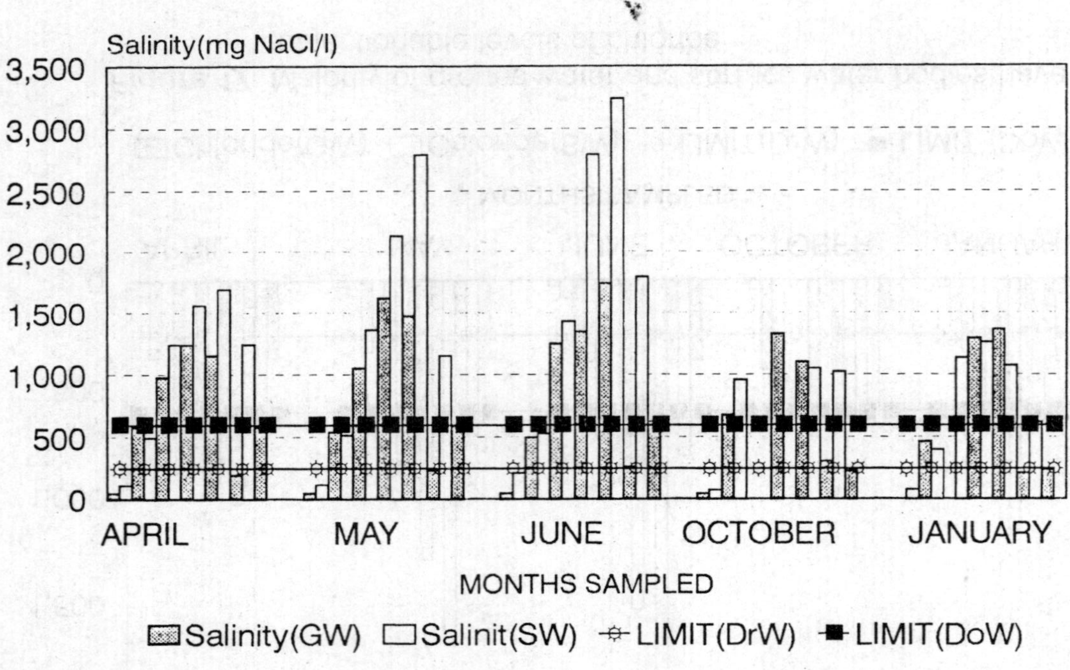

Figure 18. In most of the samples sodium chloride contents are surpassing the limits even for drinking water

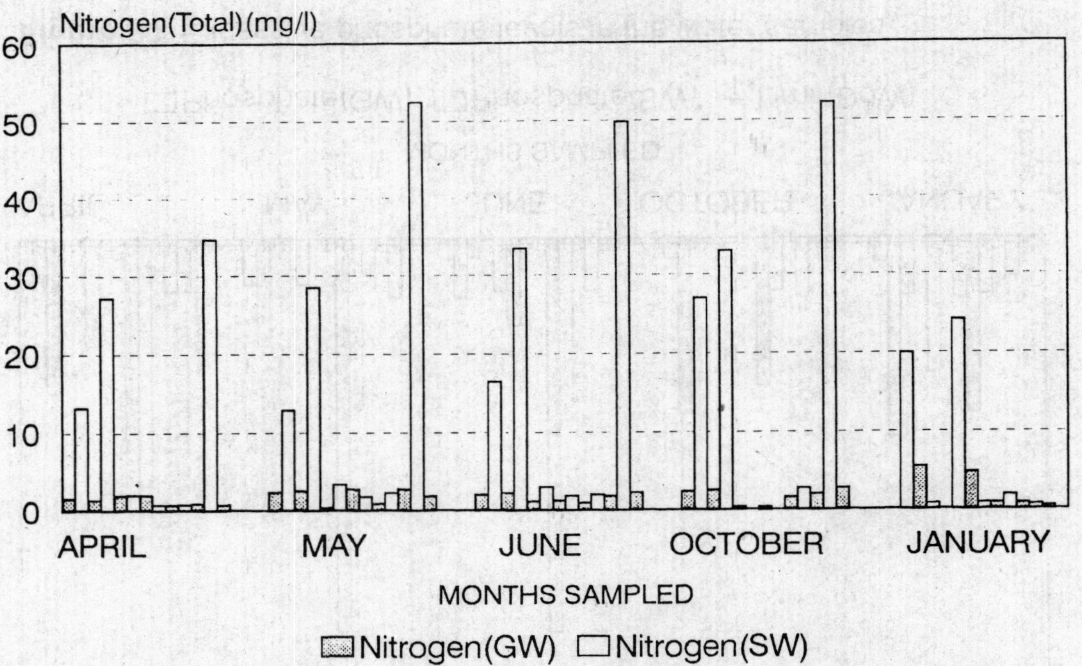

Figure 19. Nitrogen levels in the water samples

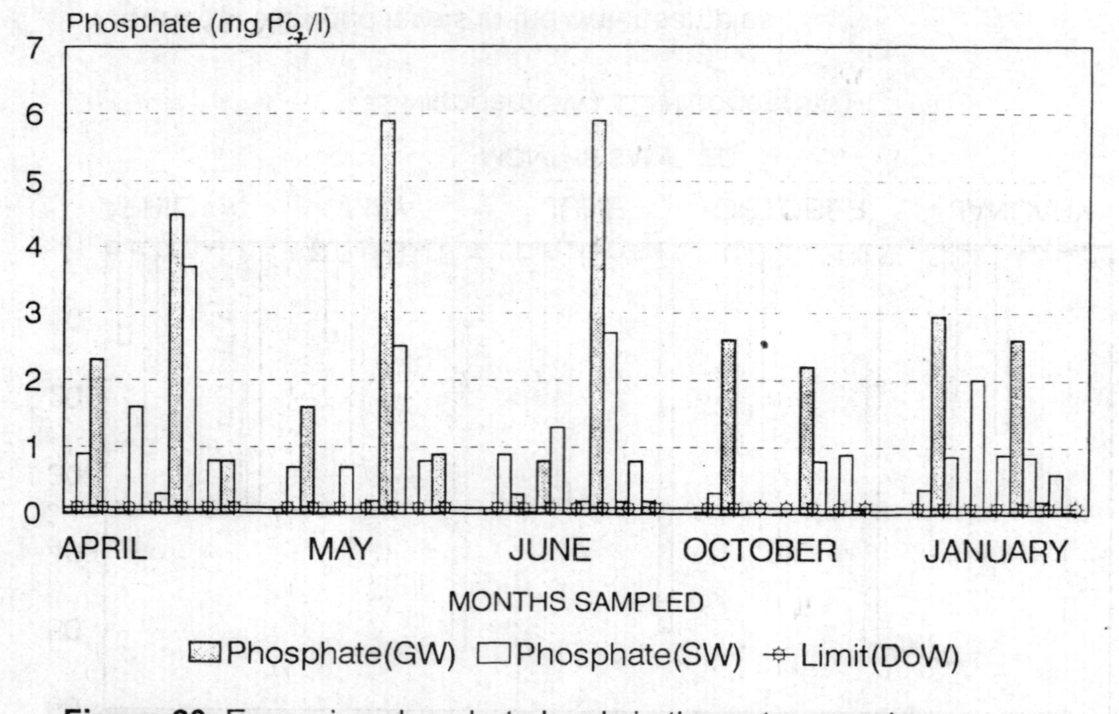

Figure 20. Excessive phosphate levels in the water samples

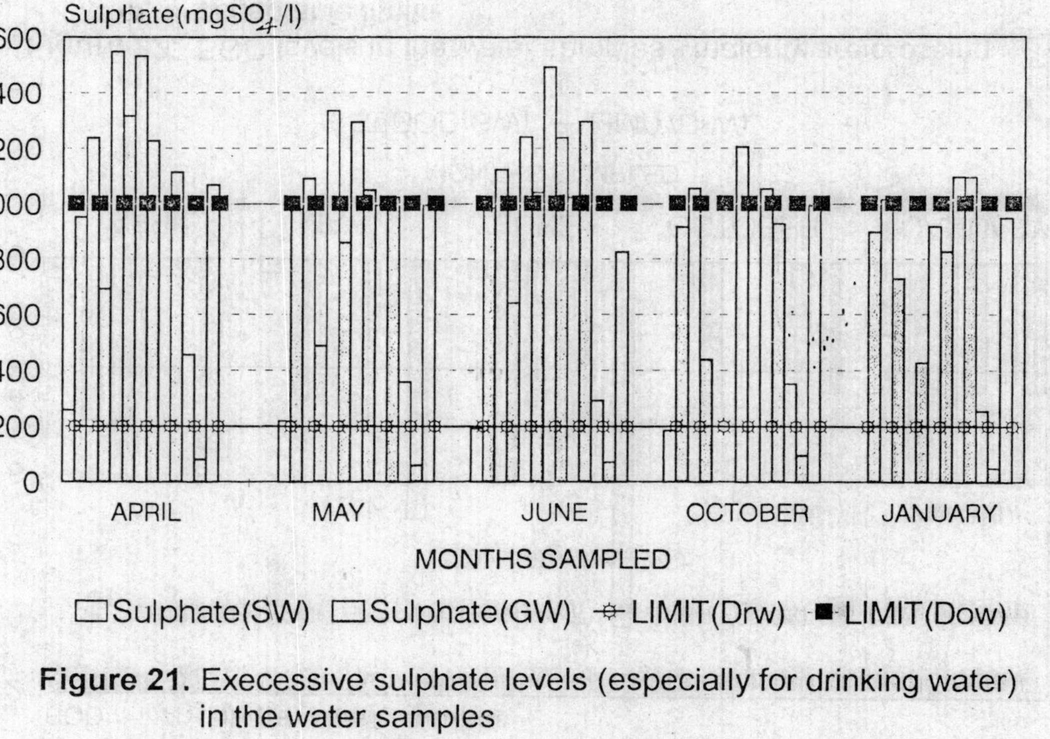

Figure 21. Execessive sulphate levels (especially for drinking water) in the water samples

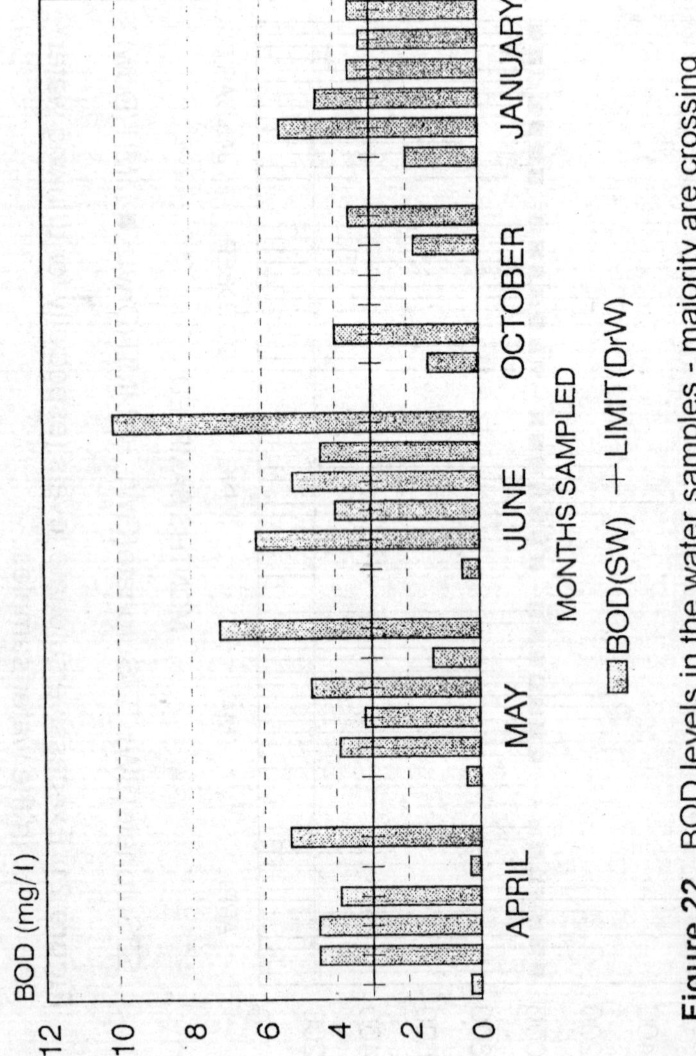

Figure 22. BOD levels in the water samples - majority are crossing acceptable limits

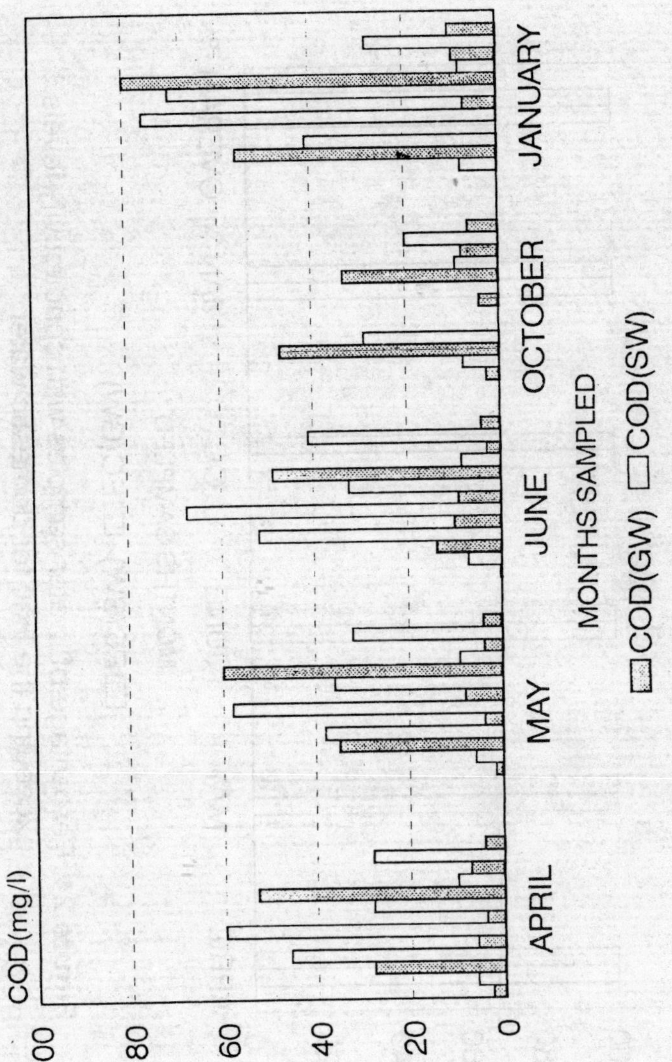

Figure 23. COD levels in the water samples

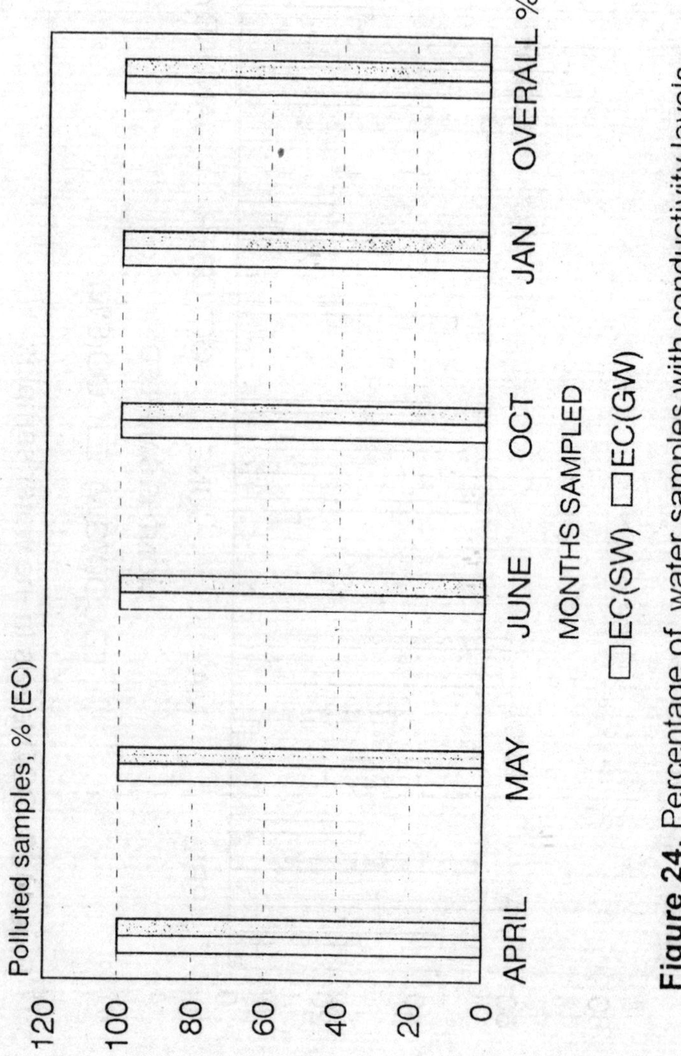

Figure 24. Percentage of water samples with conductivity levels exceeding the limit for domestic water

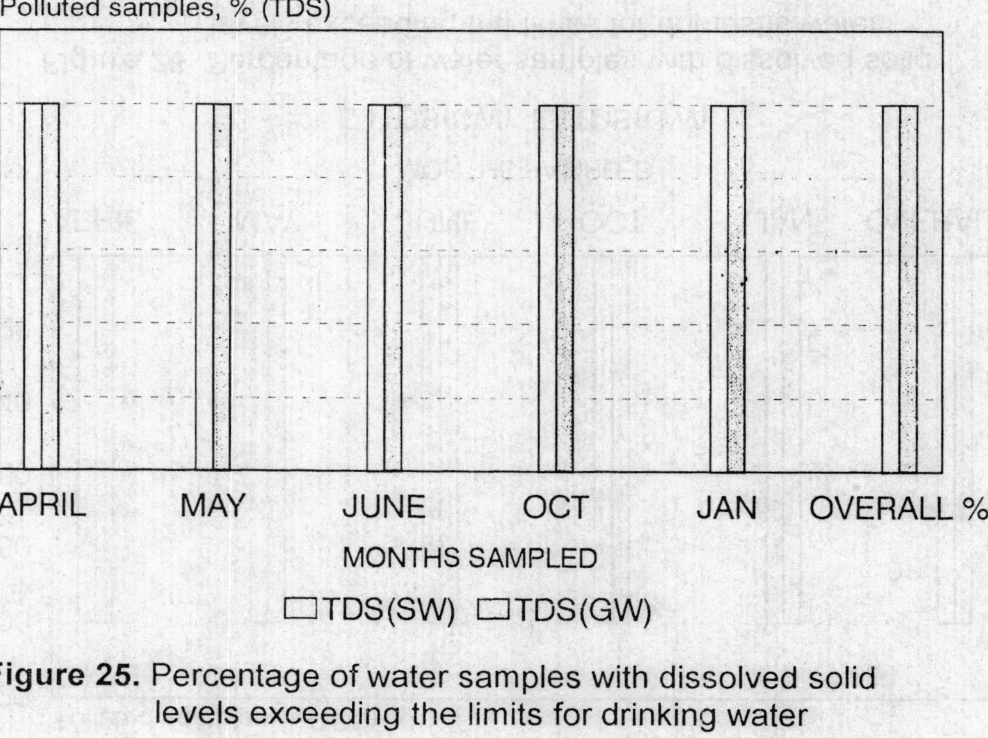

Figure 25. Percentage of water samples with dissolved solid levels exceeding the limits for drinking water

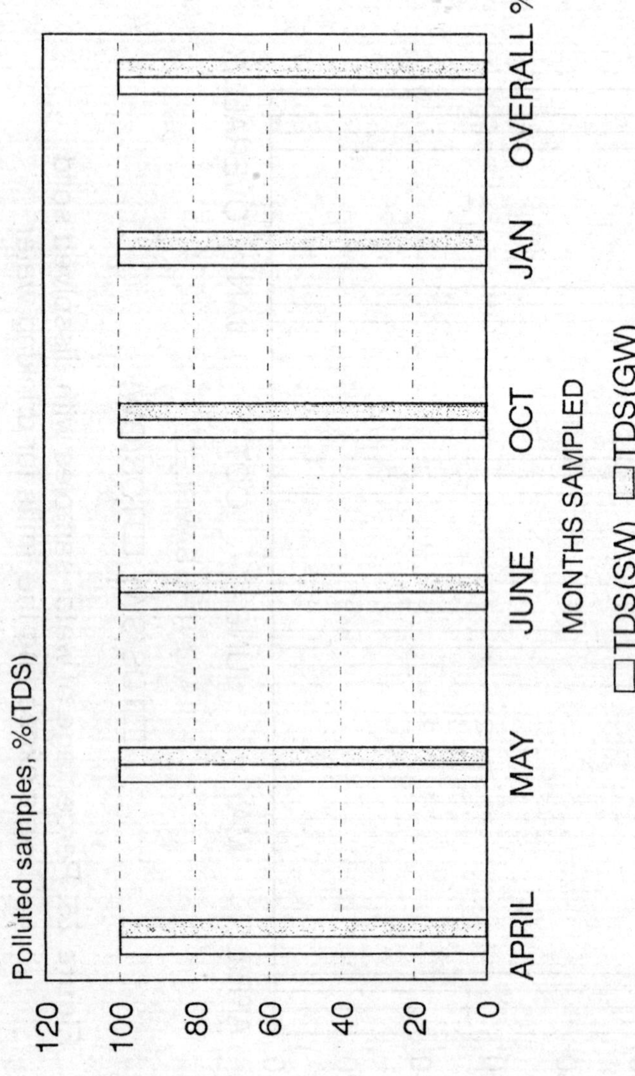

Figure 26. Percentage of water samples with dissolved solid levels exceeding the limits for domestic water

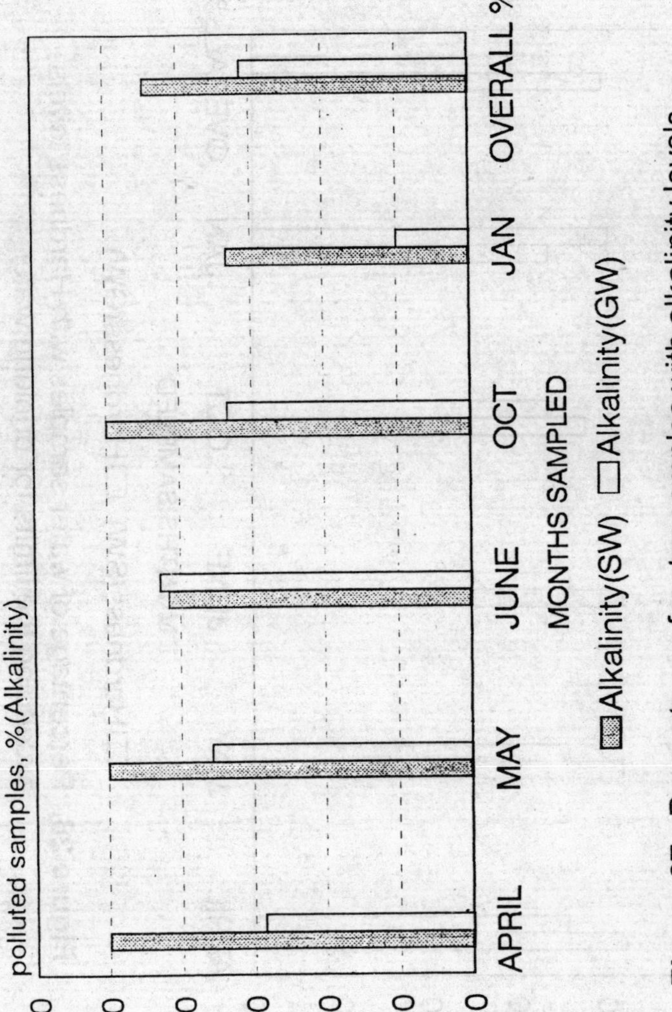

Figure 27. Percentage of water samples with alkalinity levels exceeding the limit for drinking water

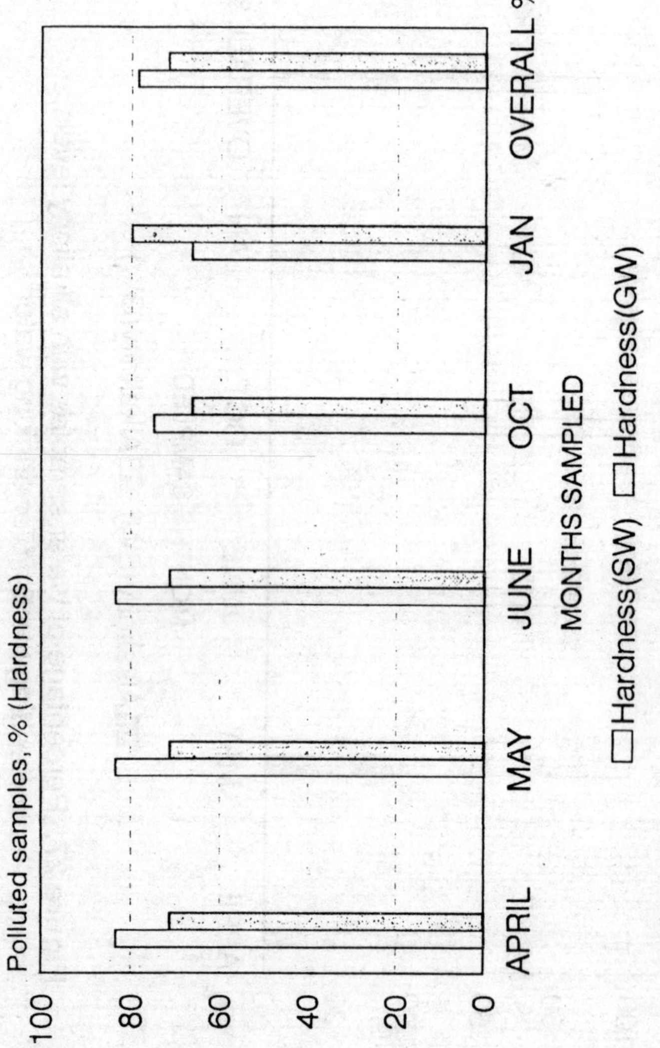

Figure 28. Percentage of water samples with Hardness levels exceeding the limits for drinking water

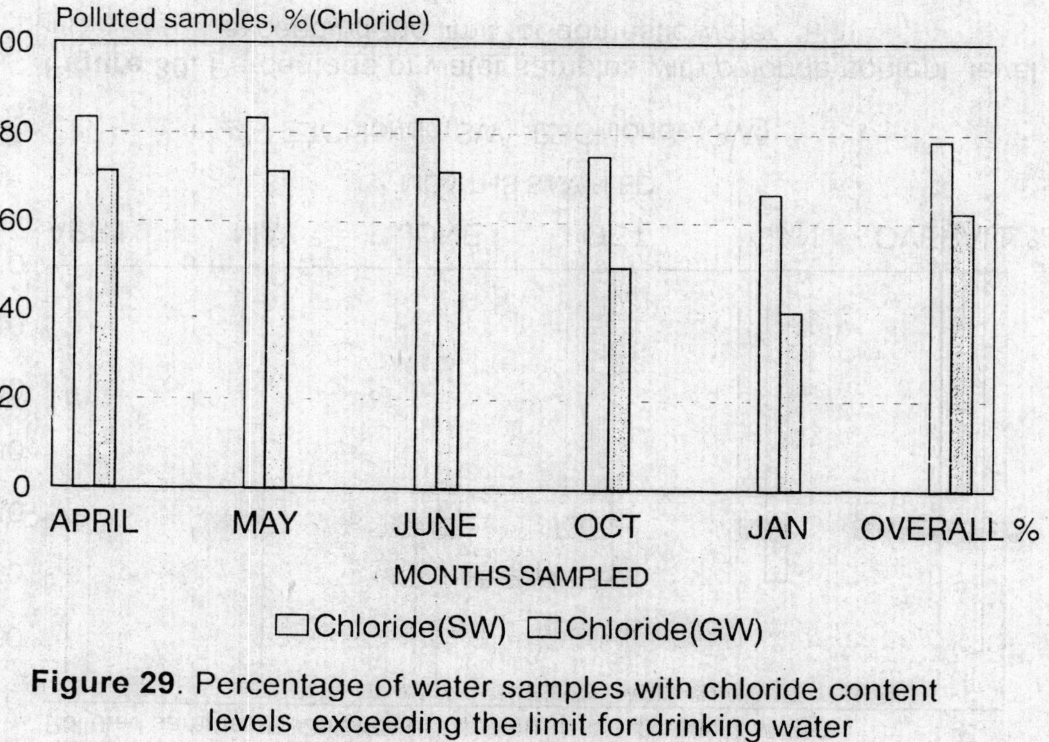

Figure 29. Percentage of water samples with chloride content levels exceeding the limit for drinking water

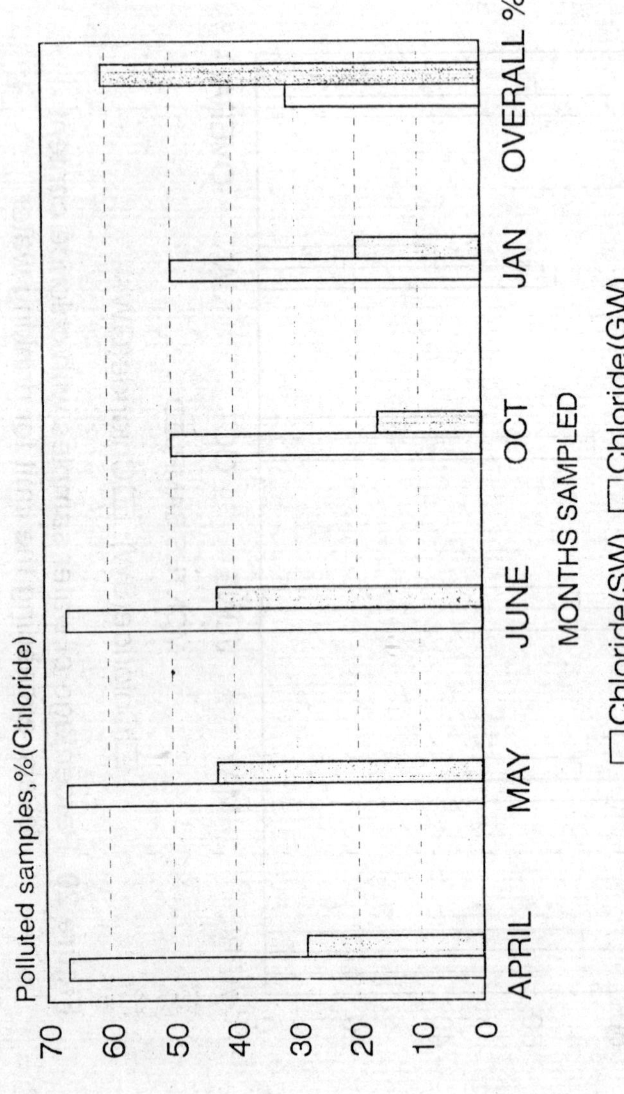

Figure 30. Percentage of water samples with chloride content level exceeding the limit for domestic water

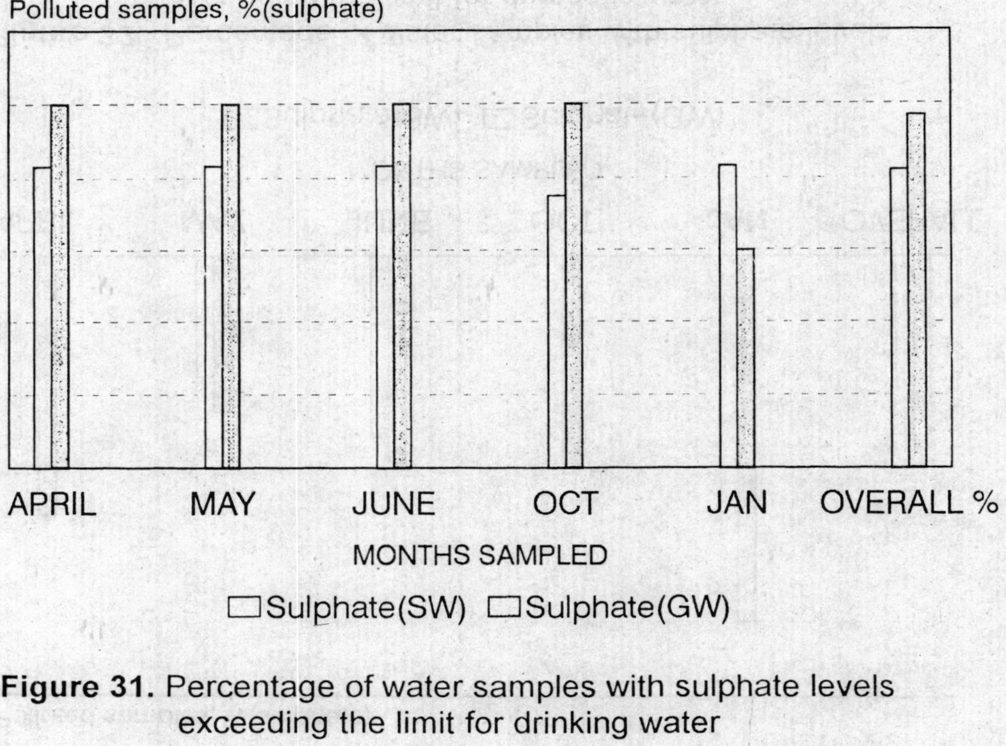

Figure 31. Percentage of water samples with sulphate levels exceeding the limit for drinking water

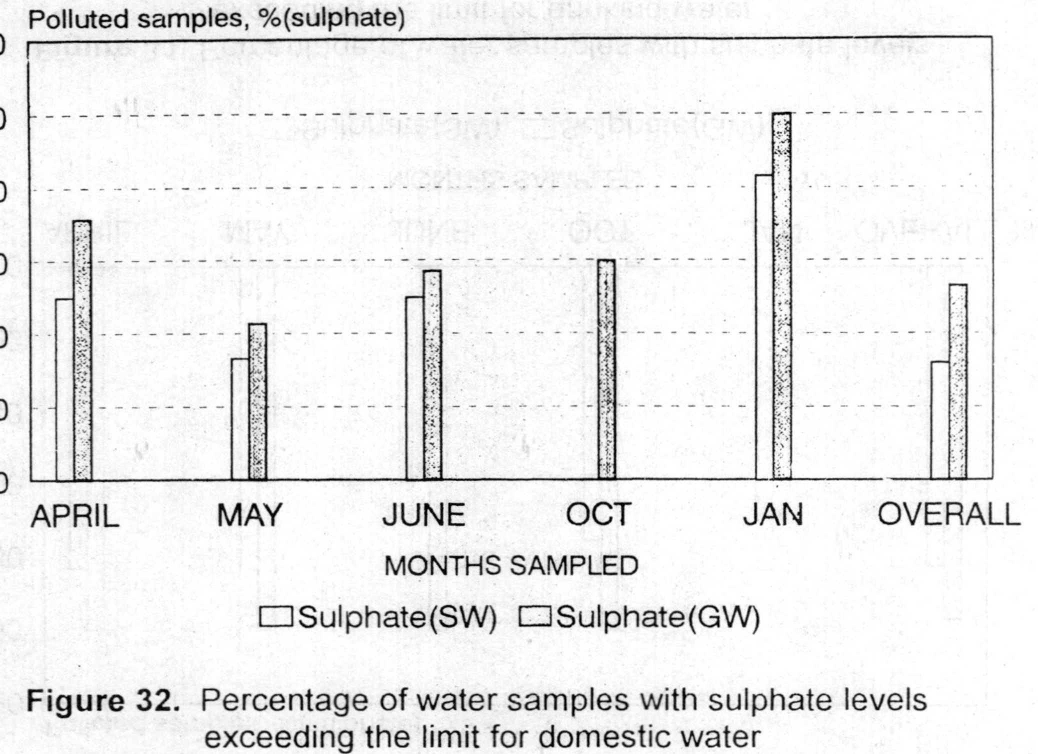

Figure 32. Percentage of water samples with sulphate levels exceeding the limit for domestic water

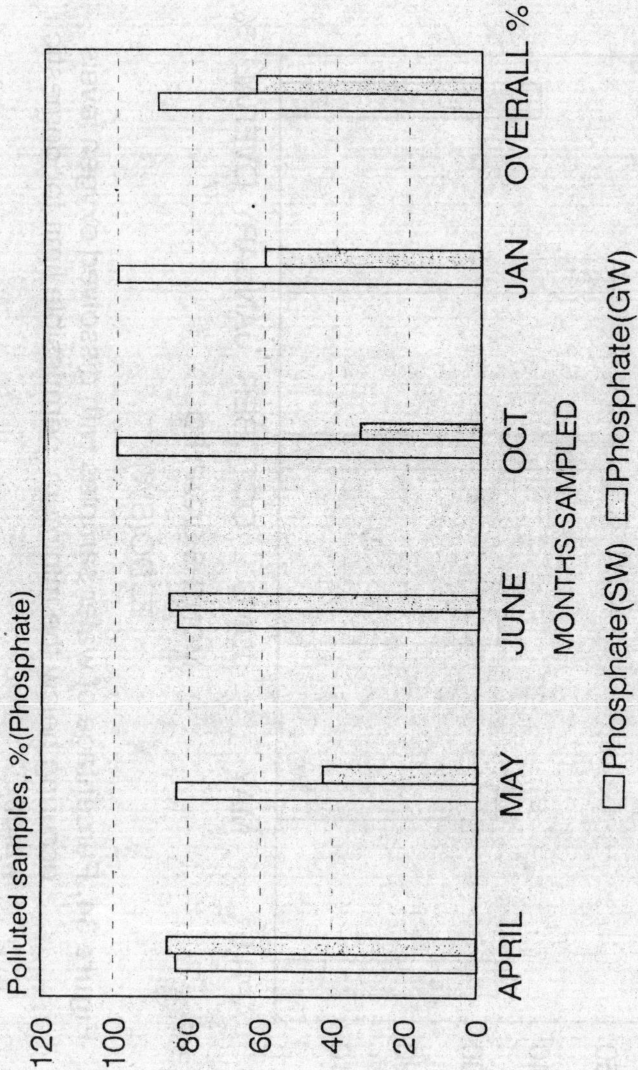

Figure 33. Percentage of water samples with phosphate levels exceeding the limit for domestic water

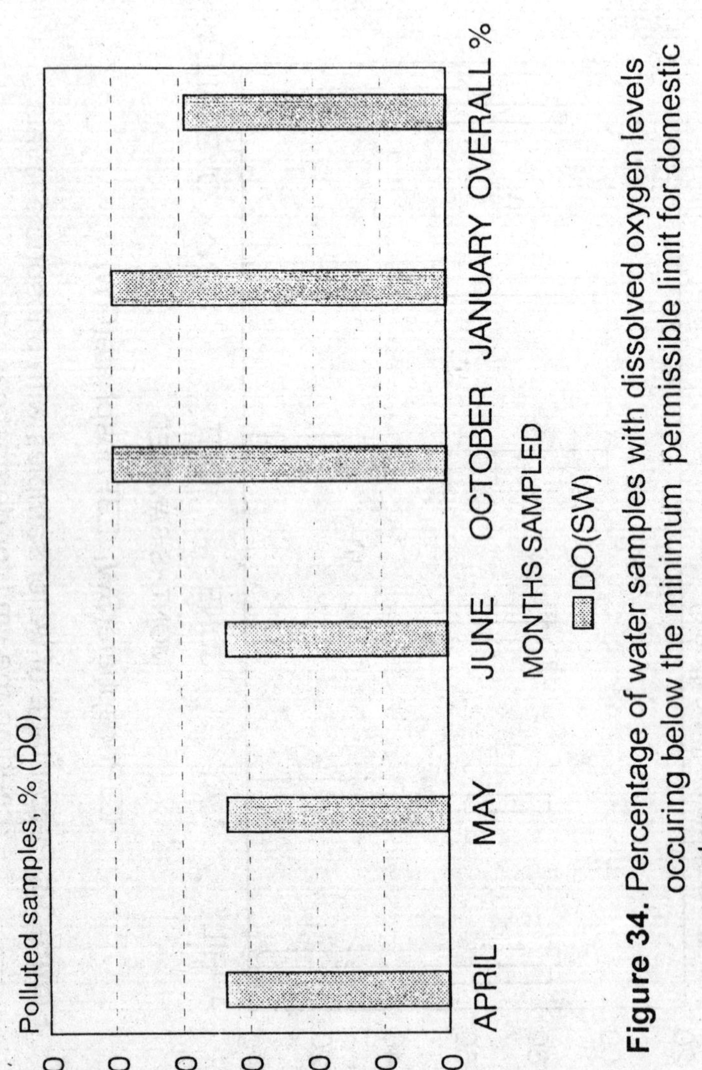

Figure 34. Percentage of water samples with dissolved oxygen levels occuring below the minimum permissible limit for domestic water

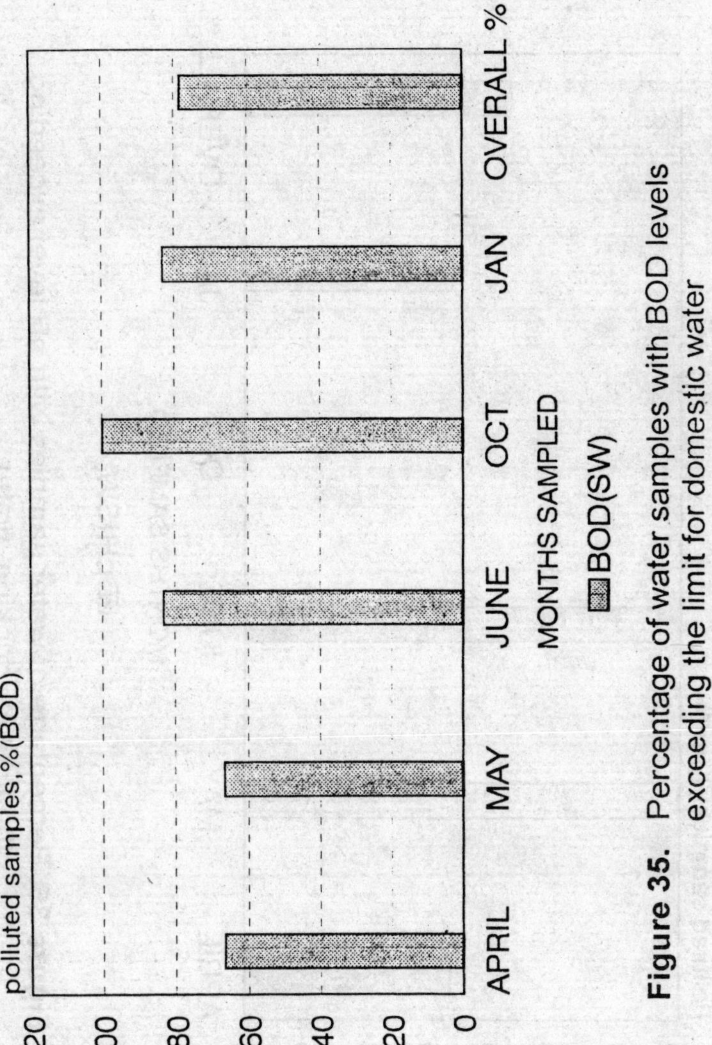

Figure 35. Percentage of water samples with BOD levels exceeding the limit for domestic water

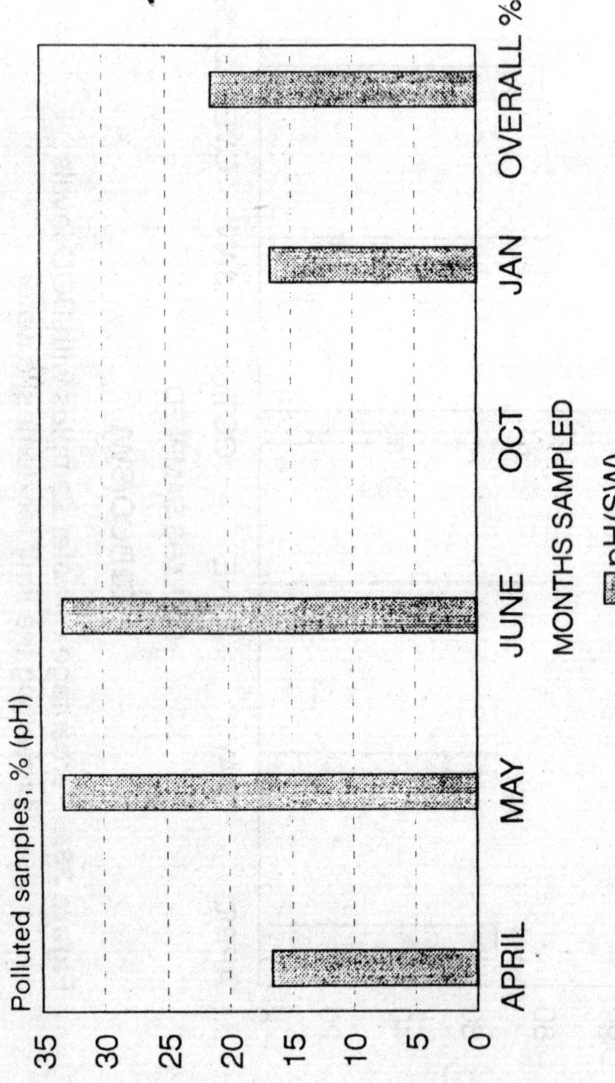

Figure 36. Percentage of water samples with pH level exceeding the limit for drinking water

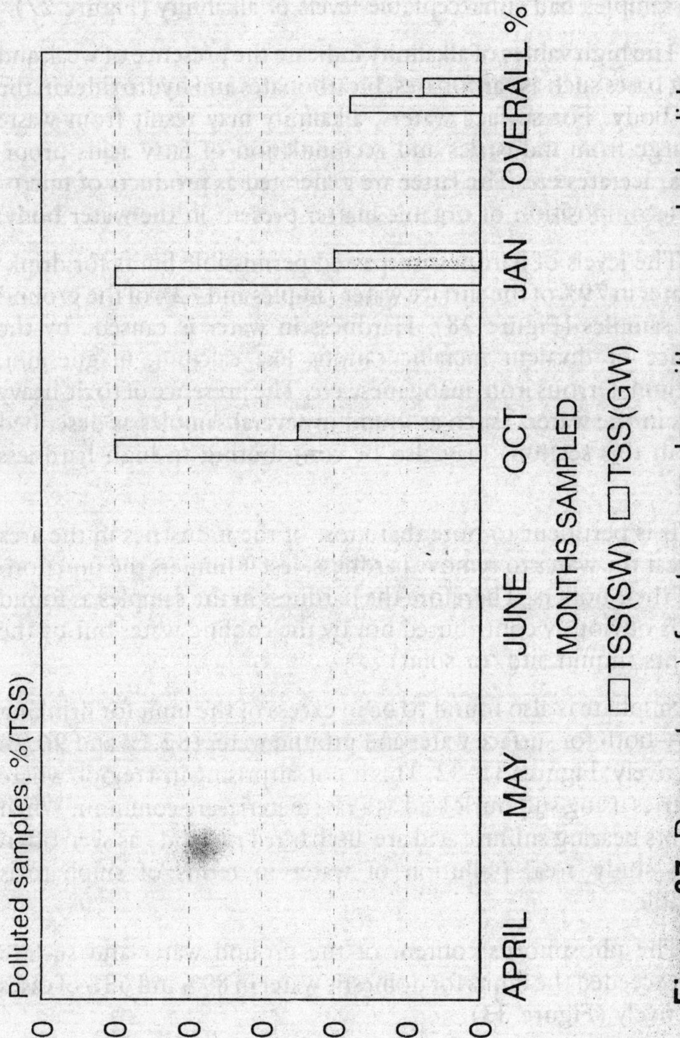

Figure 37. Percentage of water samples with suspended solid content exceeding the limits for domestic water

surpassing the permissible limits in most cases. Eightynine percent of the surface water samples had alkalinity levels crossing the permissible limit for drinking water. Likewise 63% of the groundwater samples had unacceptable levels of alkalinity (Figure 27).

The high values of alkalinity indicate the presence of weak and strong bases such as carbonates, bicarbonates and hydroxides in the water body. For surface waters, alkalinity may result from waste discharge from industries and accumulation of fatty acids propionates, acetates *etc.* The latter are generated as products of microbial decomposition of organic matter present in the water body.

The levels of hardness surpassed permissible limits for drinking water in 79% of the surface water samples and 72% of the ground water samples (Figure 28). Hardness in water is caused by the presence of divalent metallic cations like calcium, magnesium, strontium, ferrous iron, manganese *etc.* The presence of toxic heavy metals in the waters (such as found in several samples as described latter in this section) may also be contributing to high hardness values.

It is pertinent to note that most of the industries in the area pre-treat the water to remove hardness, lest it hinders the functioning of their boilers. Therefore the hardness in the samples as found by us is obviously contributed not by the cooling water but by the effluents (liquid and/or solid).

Sulphate is also found to be in excess of the limit for drinking water—both for surface water and ground water (82.1% and 96.9% respectively) Figures 31–32. This is not surprising in a region where industries using sulphuric acid as a raw material are common. When effluents bearing sulfuric acid are discharged on land - as seen often in the study area, pollution of water in terms of sulphate is inevitable.

The phosphorus content of the ground water and surface water exceeded the limits for domestic water in 89% and 63% of cases respectively (Figure 33).

For 40% of the samples, the DO level is below the minimum permissible level for domestic water (Figure 34) whereas in 79% of the samples the BOD is exceeding the limits for domestic water (Figure 35). These findings indicate contribution of biodegradable pollutants, presumably from pulp and paper industries.

In 100% of the surface water samples total suspended solids (TSS) were above the permissible level during the monsoon and post monsoon periods (Figure 37); this may be due to solid wastes getting washed into water bodies with the rainwater.

Presence of Highly Toxic Elements

A particularly alarming finding is the presence of excessive concentrations of such toxic elelments as arsenic and mercury in water (Table 3.33 and Figures 38–46). *Mercury was found in concentrations 150 to 1100 times higher than the permissible limit for drinking water. The concentrations of arsenic, mercury, iron, manganese and cadmium was found to be crossing the permissible levels for drinking water in 100% cases (Figure 3.45). Arsenic, cadmium and manganese (for surface water) were also found to be present at levels higher than allowable for irrigation water in 100% cases (Figure 3.46).*

Sources of Pollution

The pollution of the water environment, quantified by the above mentioned findings, may be due to:

a) heavy withdrawal of ground water leading to salinity intrusion;

b) pollution of aquifers and surface water bodies due to industrial effluents.

Evidence of both types of impacts has been found by us. Surveys revealed that barely 11 years ago many of the now salinized wells were usable. After the establishment of industries during the 1980s and the consequent spurt in groundwater extraction, the salinity intrusion began and in a few years several wells became saline (Figure 47). This was seriously aggravated by the pollution caused by industries in the form of :

a) effluent discharged in ponds and on land and

b) run-off from the solid waste dumps.

These have polluted the surface water bodies which, being rain-fed, would not otherwise have become saline. Subsequently,

Table 33. Heavy Metal Contents of Water Samples

S.No.	Metals*	Months Sampled				
		April '94	May '94	June '94	Oct. '94	Jan. '95
		Ground Water				
1.	Arsenic	0.125	0.334	0.125	0.182	0.377
2.	Cadmium	0.102	0.109	0.236	0.181	0.085
3.	Iron	7.285	4.985	6.251	0.969	0.707
4.	Manganese	0.184	0.216	--	0.272	0.630
5.	Mercury	0.384	0.360	0.473	0.530	0.263
6.	Nickel	0.109	0.119	0.081	0.174	0.020
7.	Zinc	0.330	0.474	1.652	1.032	0.380
		Surface Water				
1.	Arsenic	0.125	0.228	0.192	0.242	0.314
2.	Cadmium	0.082	0.098	0.251	0.150	0.094
3.	Iron	1.663	1.238	3.021	0.455	2.073
4.	Manganese	0.554	0.608		0.208	0.883
5.	Mercury	0.293	0.165	0.284	1.116	0.946
6.	Nickel	0.080	0.091	0.057	0.104	0.153
7.	Zinc	0.197	0.147	3.336	0.398	0.298

* *All units are in mg/l*

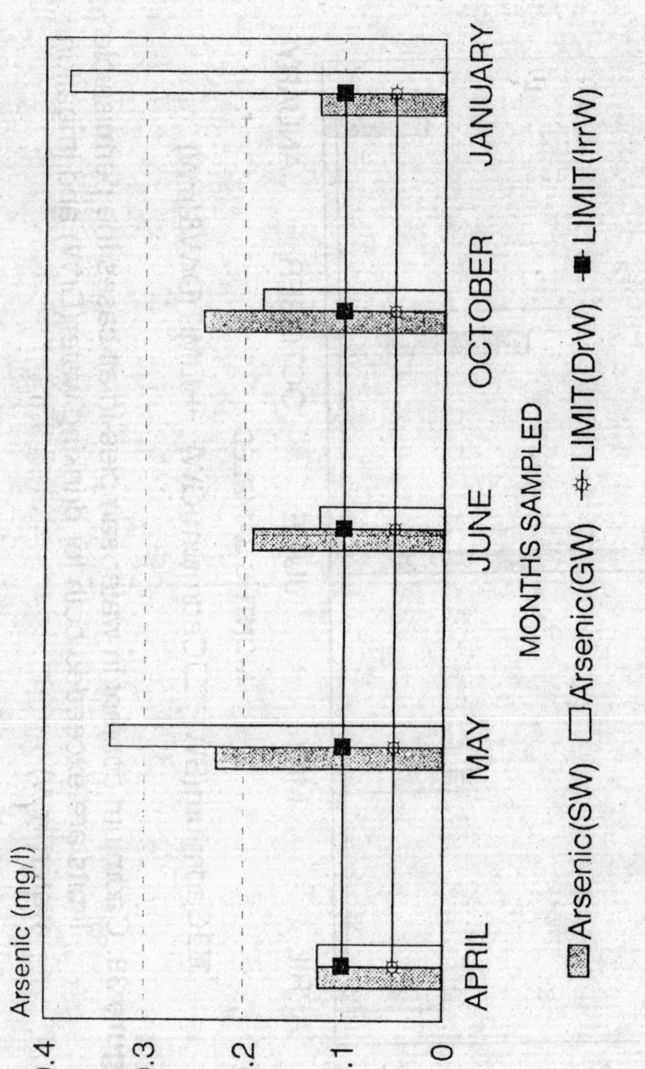

Figure 38. Arsenic content in water samples - in all cases the permissible limits are exceeded both for drinking water(DrW) and irrigation water(IrrW)

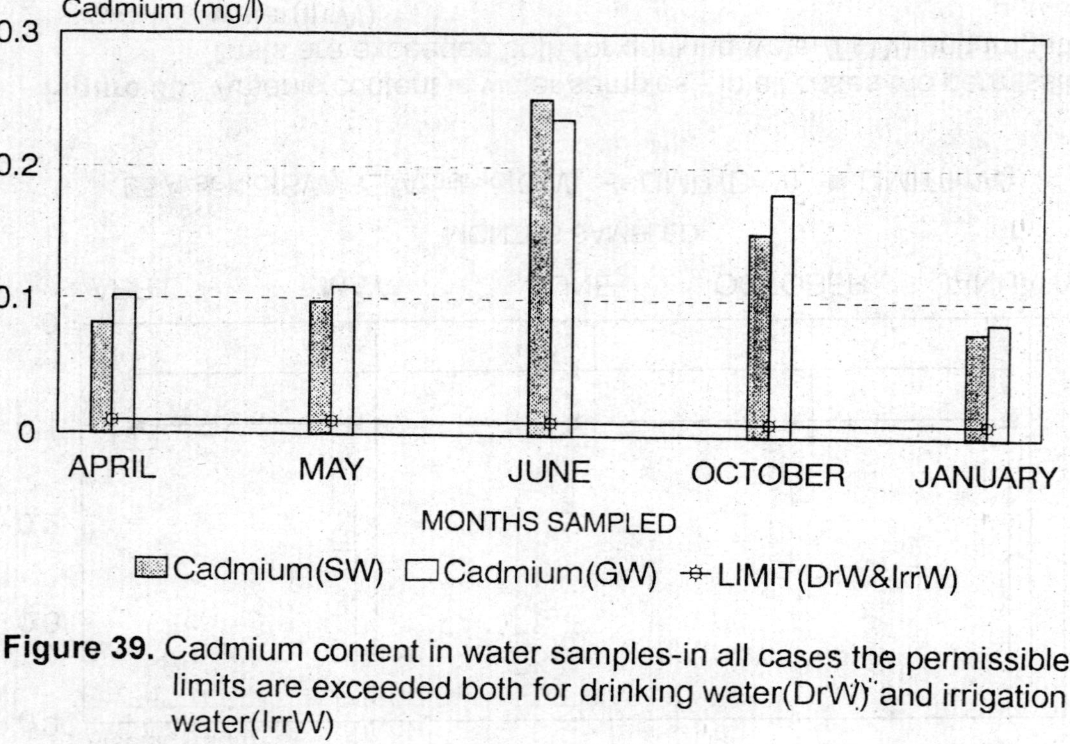

Figure 39. Cadmium content in water samples-in all cases the permissible limits are exceeded both for drinking water(DrW) and irrigation water(IrrW)

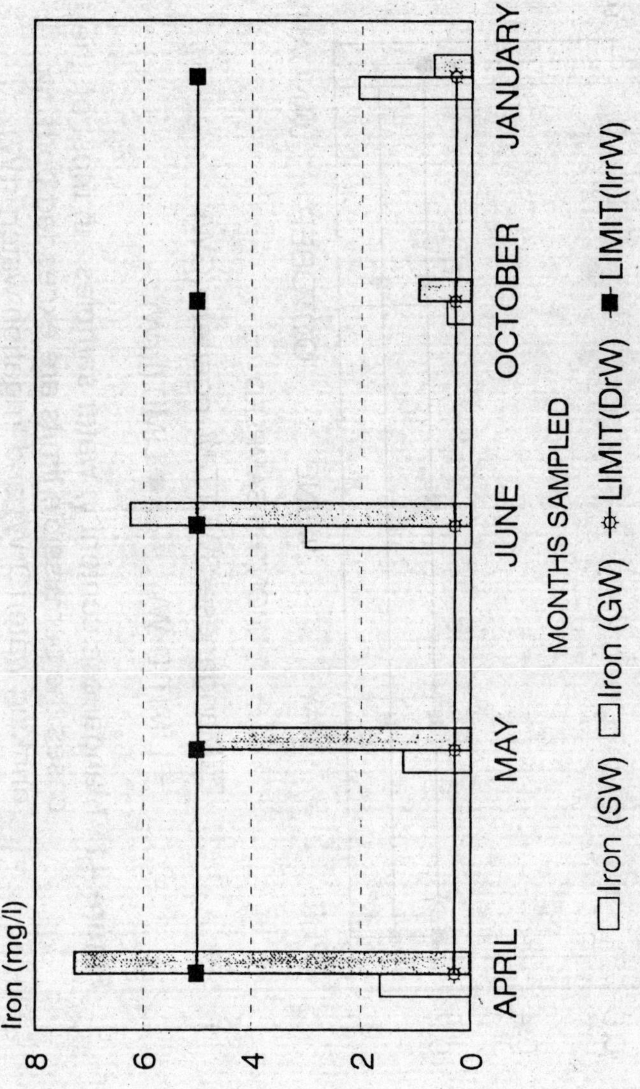

Figure 40. Iron content in water samples - all samples are unfit for drinking and several for irrigation too

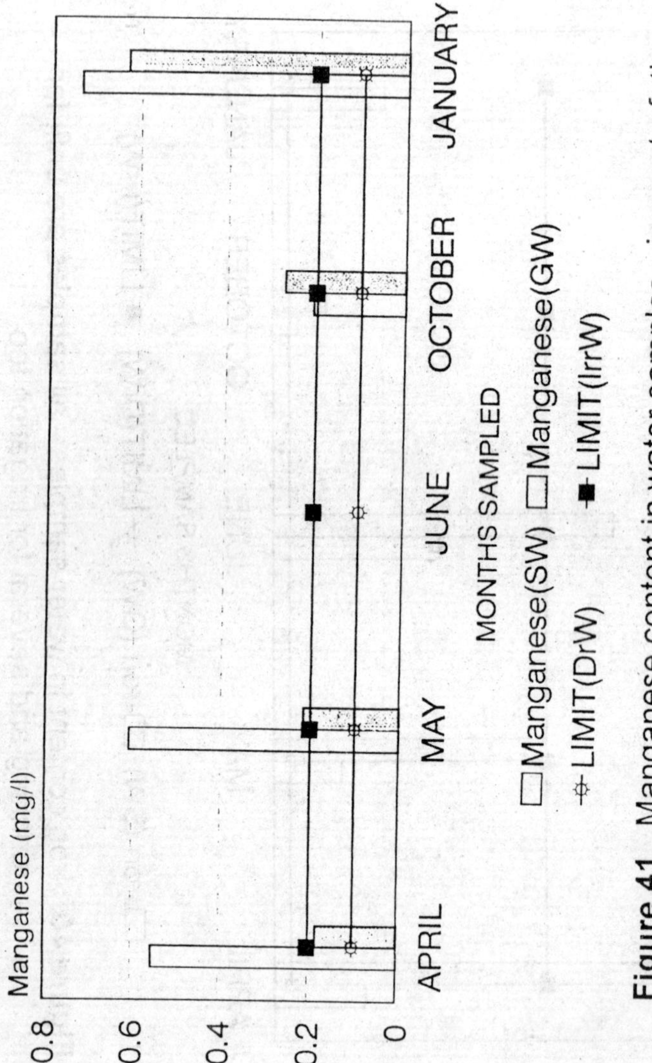

Figure 41. Manganese content in water samples - in most of the cases the permissible limits are exceeded both for drinking water(DrW) and irrigation water(IrrW)

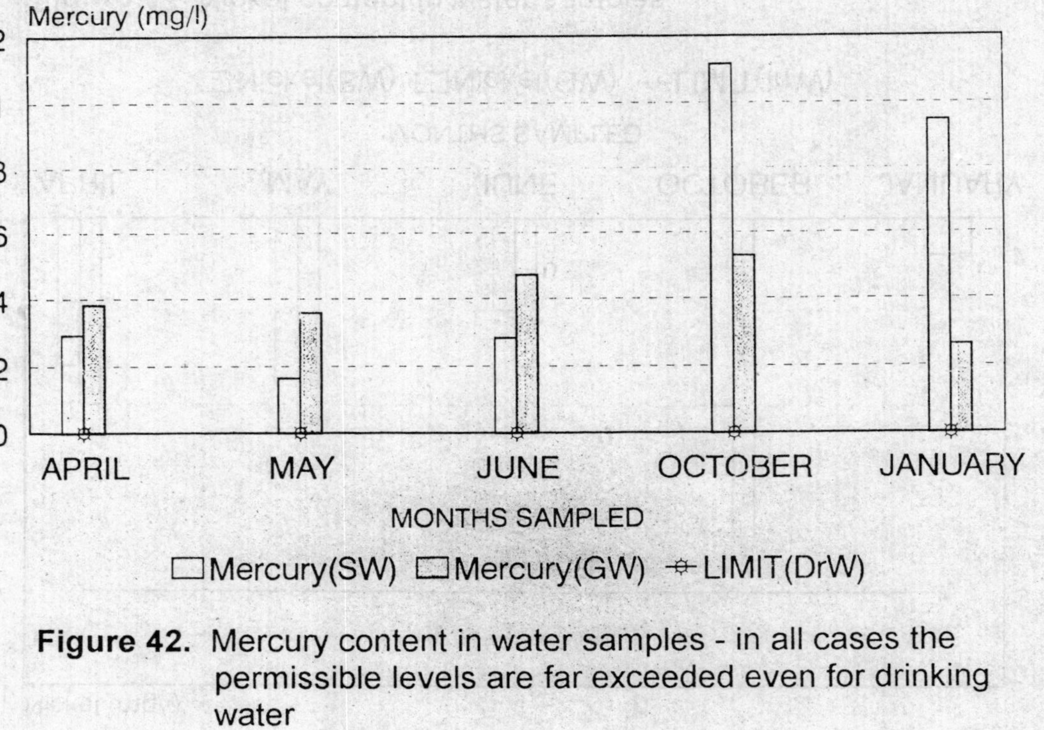

Figure 42. Mercury content in water samples - in all cases the permissible levels are far exceeded even for drinking water

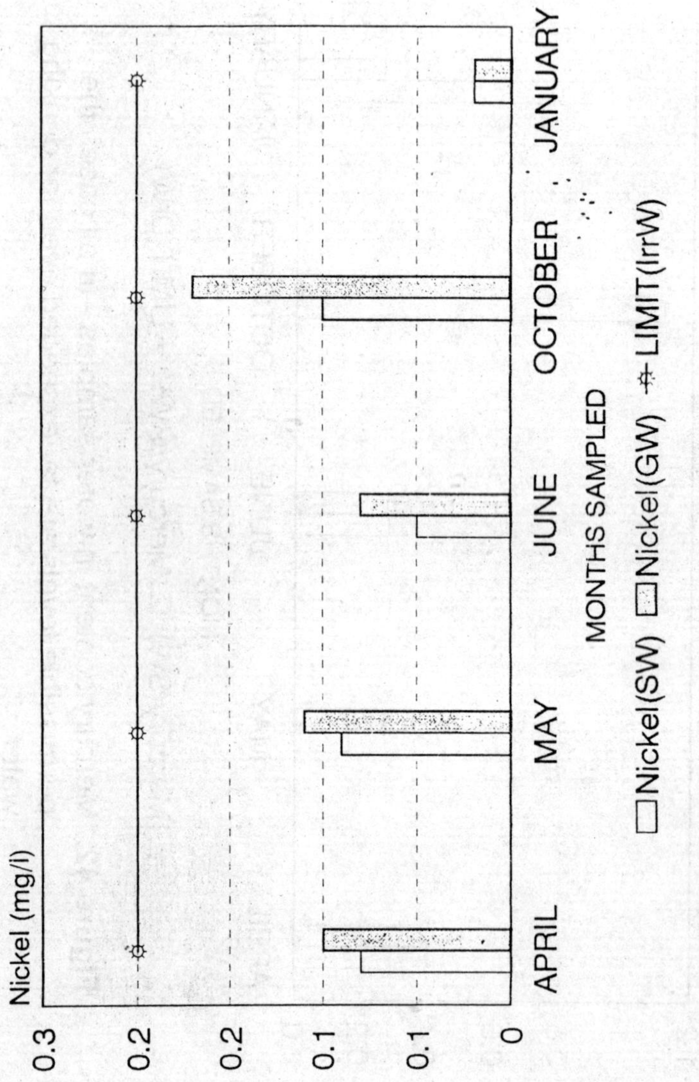

Figure 43. Nickel content in water samples

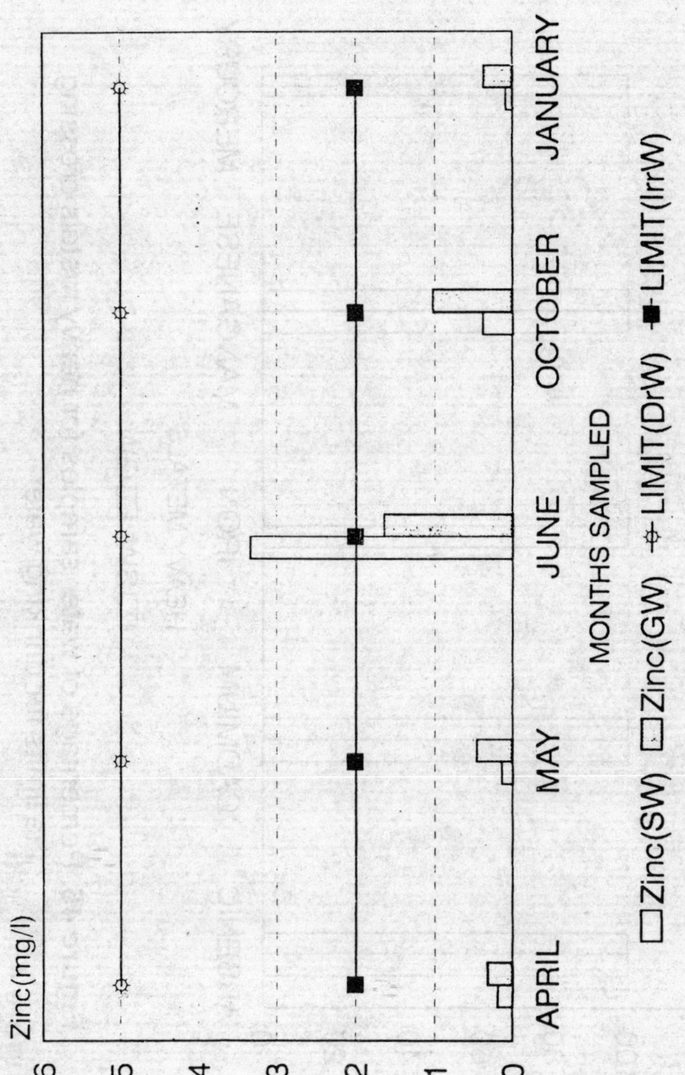

Figure 44. Zinc content in water samples

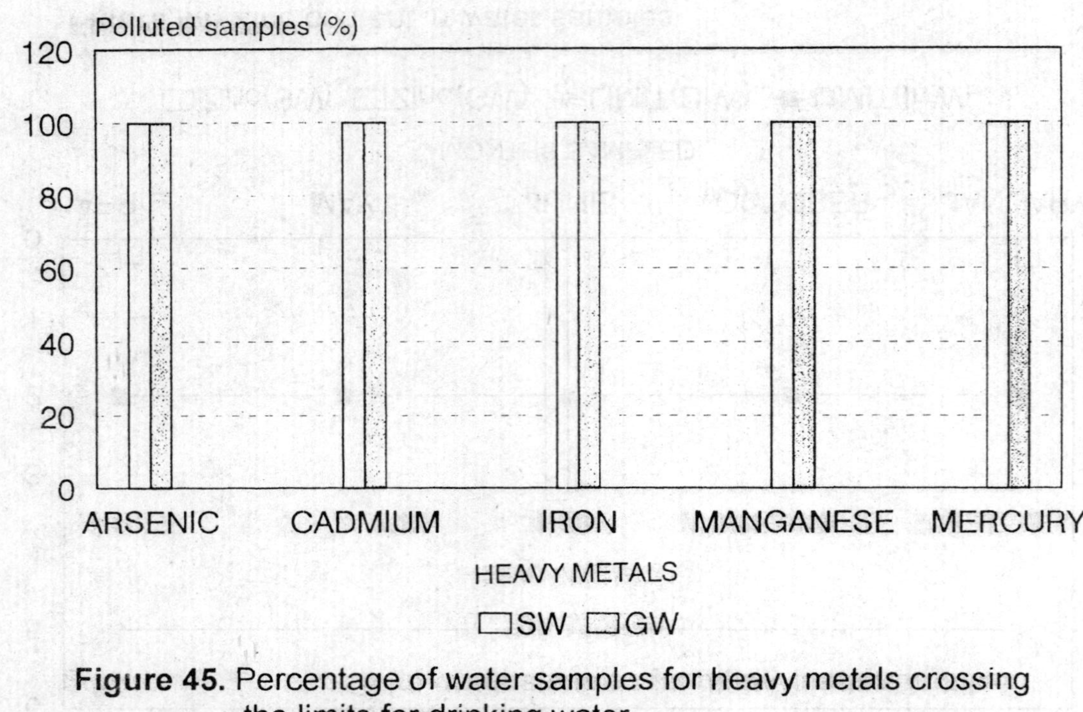

Figure 45. Percentage of water samples for heavy metals crossing the limits for drinking water

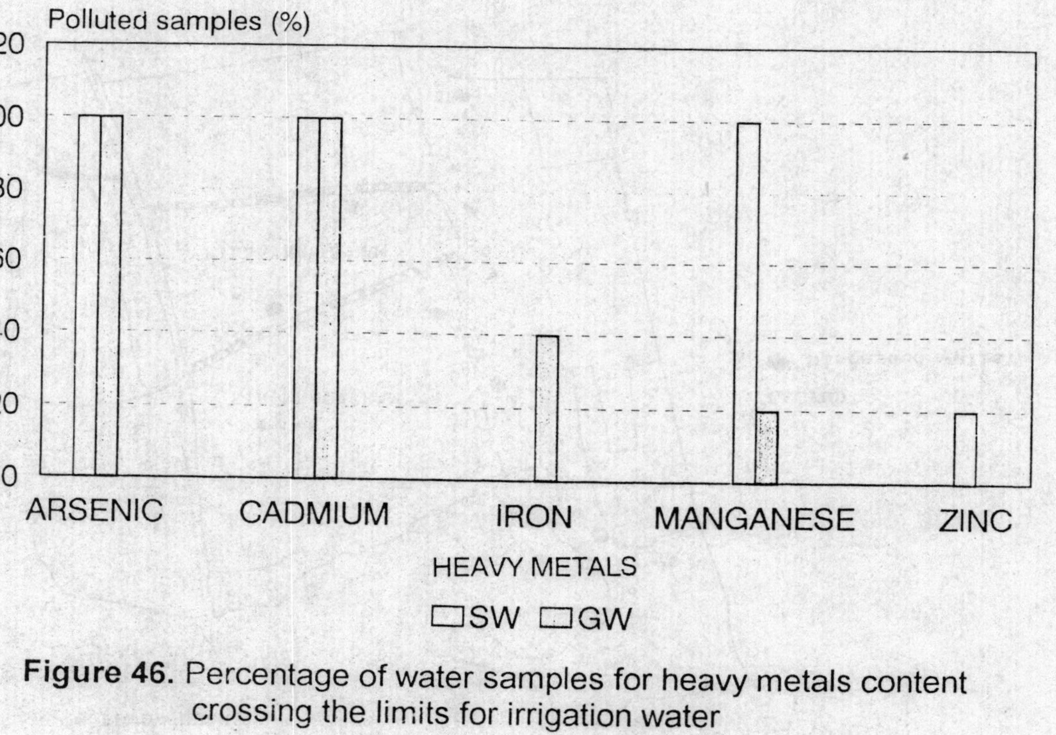

Figure 46. Percentage of water samples for heavy metals content crossing the limits for irrigation water

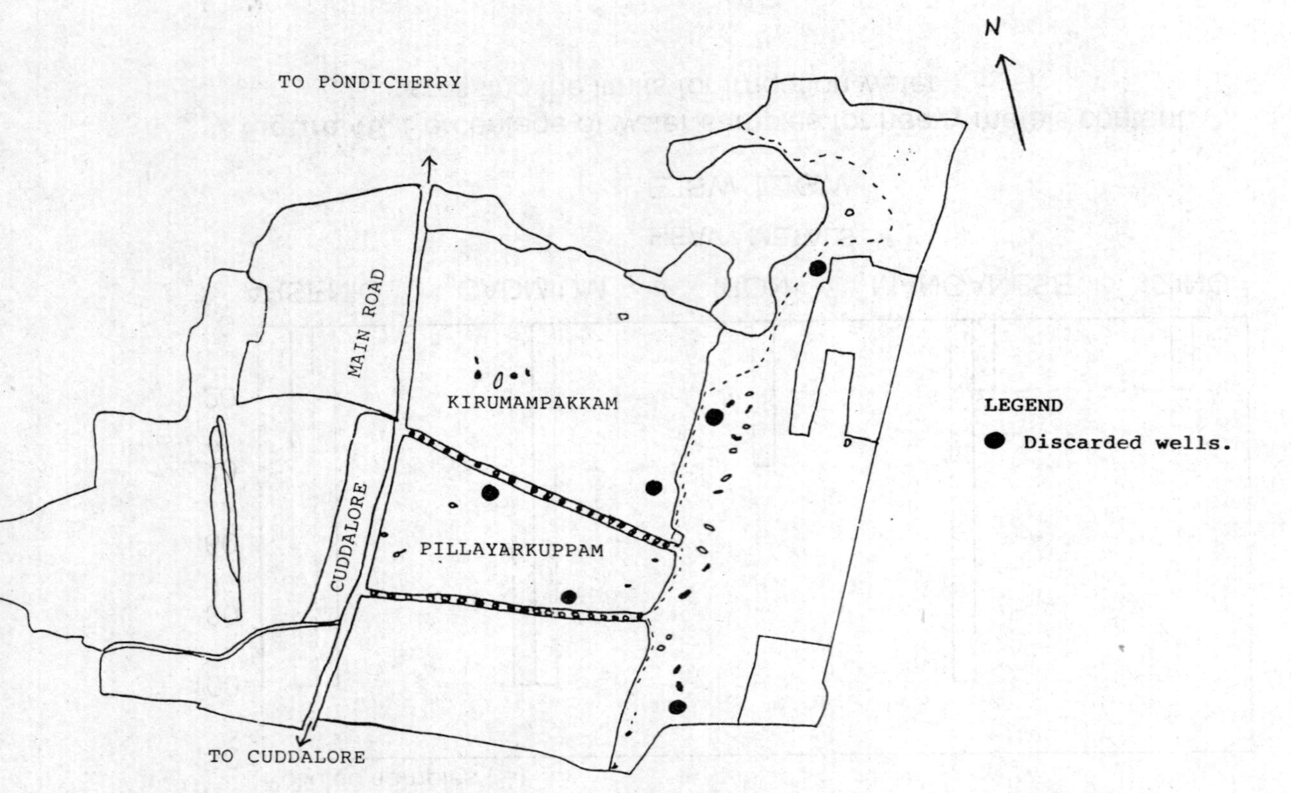

Figure 47. Map showing the location of the unused wells of the study area due to salinity intrusion

through infiltration, the groundwater has also become contaminated. The contribution from the agriculture and domestic spheres can be ignored due to their minor nature and compared to industrial usage in terms of number of consumers and volume/quantity consumed.

The abandoned borewells and hand-pumps depict the plight of the villagers due to the salinized and polluted ground water in this region. Some of the surface water bodies and the wells which were once used for bathing, irrigation and fishing have even disappeared. The process of sea-water intrusion continues, exposing more and more parts of the aquifer to irrepairable damage. By now wells situated upto a kilometer away from the sea-coast have become salinized (Figures 48–49); the extent of salinity intrusion is greater near the coast and decreases almost linearly as one moves inland. Similar situation of well water becoming saline has also been reported (Olaniya *et al*, 1969) in other typical industrial area.

The fact that parameters like sulphate, hardness, chloride, EC and TDS are high not solely because of salinity intrusion but due to the combination of industrial pollution and salinity intrusion (catalysed by excessive water withdrawal by the industries) is borne out by statistical analysis of water quality data (Manual for statistical analysis and interpretation of water quality data, 1987). Multiple regression between different parameters (presented in Annexure III and IV) failed to show significant correlation, indicating that there are discrete inputs, typical of industrial sources, of wastewaters of varying characteristics into ponds and groundwater. When similar regression is performed on natural waters one invariably gets significant correlations between several parameters. The absence of correlation indicates that the ponds and underground aquifers keep receiving wastewaters of varying characteristics and concentrations—a phenomenon typical of industrial inputs (Mathew, 1982).

Similar studies reporting impact of Industrialisation on ground and surface water bodies have also been reported by many (Dhanaselvan *et al*, 1991; Rao 1993; Razia *et al*, 1990; Subramanian, 1989).

Studies on Land Environment

The studies on the impact of land-use on agriculture and the impact of solid waste dumps reveal as follows.

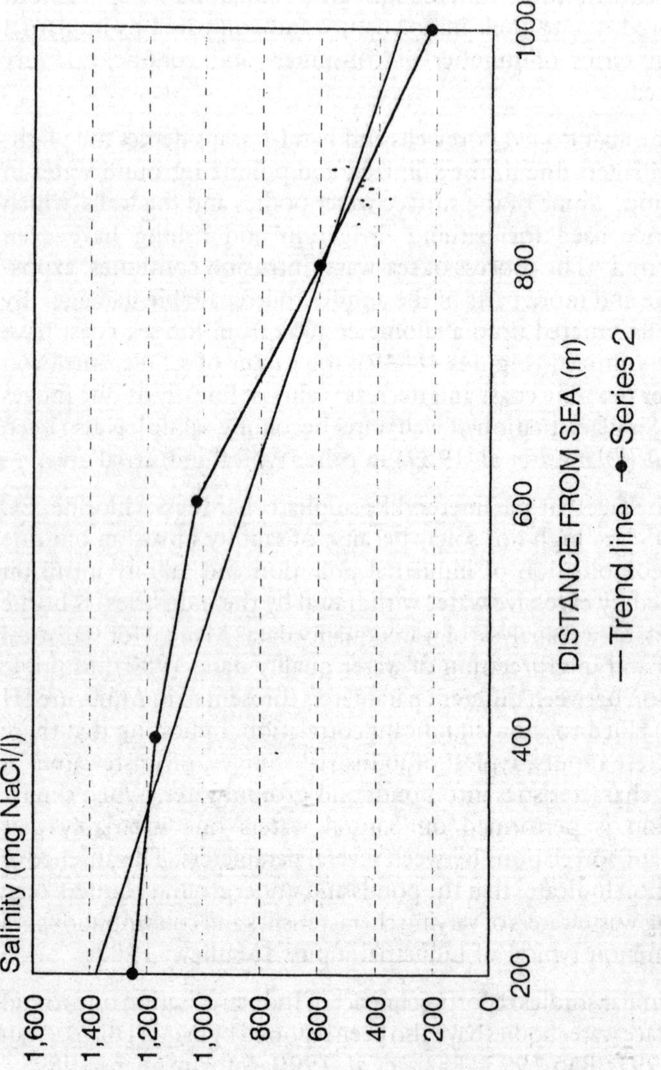

Figure 48. Salinity of well-waters as a function of distance of the wells from the sea coast

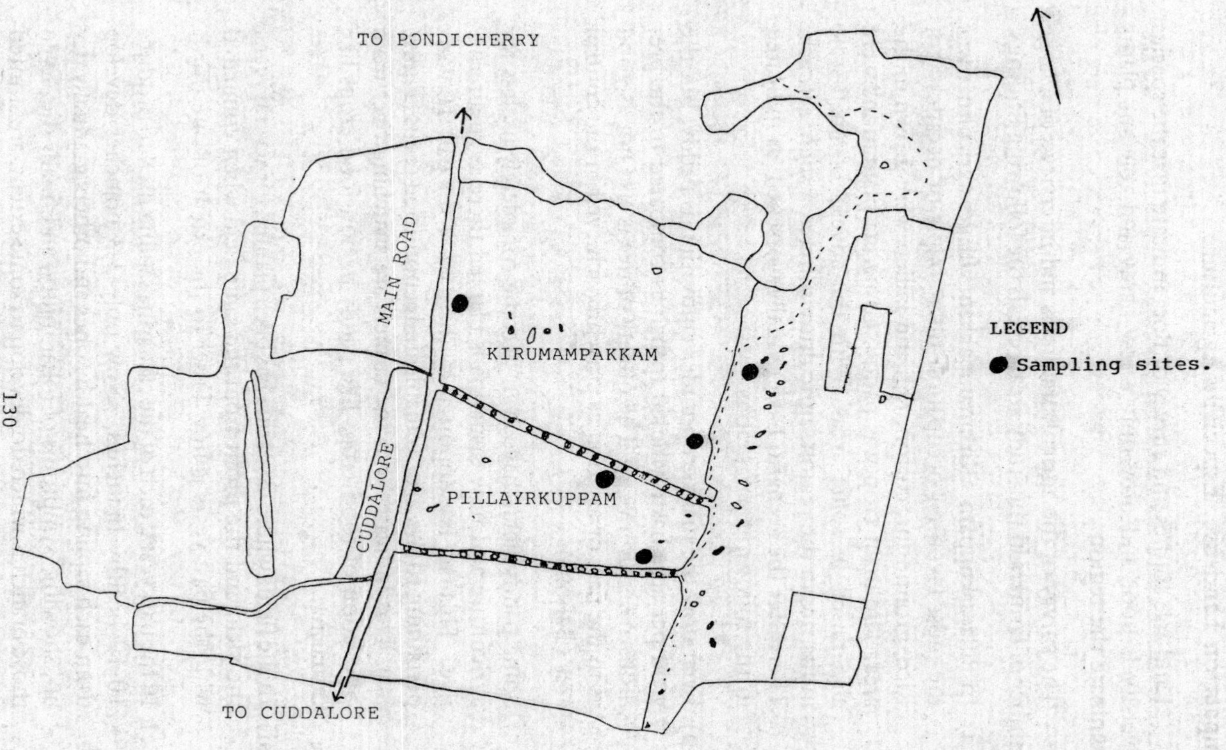

Figure 49. Map showing the sampling points for the salinity intrusion studies

130

Impact on Land-use, Especially Agriculture

Land-use studies and survey of flora indicate that the species diversity is poor and now only a few hardy and tolerant plants dominate the region.

The survey of the agricultural fields and interviews of a large number of farmers in the study area, reveals the following findings.

a) In Pillayarkuppam - Kirumampakkam villages agriculture was the most favoured occupation till a couple of decades ago. Rice, groundnut, cotton, ragi and millets were grown in the area. The main crop was paddy. Casuarina plantations were also raised in some areas. With the advent of small-scale industries in the region, agriculture suffered a *slight* setback. Thereafter the scenario has gradually worsened, as indicated in the following paragraphs.

b) Even now the main crop under cultivation is paddy, but the yield per acre has dwindled to half as compared to the pre-industrialisation years. The quality of rice is also not as good as in the past or as good as currently achieved in the control area (Bahour).

c) Some paddy fields have even become completely useless for agriculture and now casuarina is planted there as an alternative. This fact is supported by the data of the past 10 years pertaining to the area available under non-food crops (Figure 50). This indicates that the farmers are switching over from cultivation of food crops like paddy to non-food crops like casuarina.

d) In the fields where casuarina has been planted for several years, the yield and the profit from the same field when compared with the past years is now lesser to the extent of one third.

e) In the past years, each of the casuarina sapling used to produce 10-12 healthy branches. Now only 2-3 branches develop from each sapling into healthy ones and others gradually dry up, showing symptoms of foliar injury, and finally die. Even those branches which do develop to some extent, are stunted and full (normal) growth is not seen in any plant, barring a rare exception. Some areas (spanning about 20 acres) where

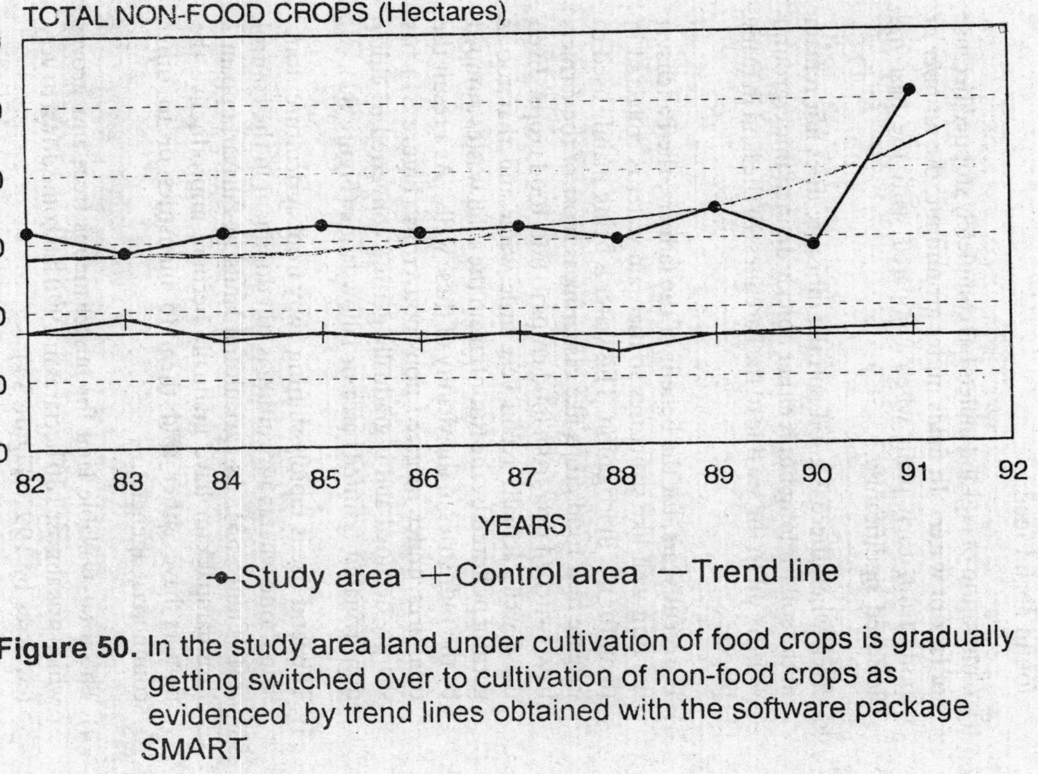

Figure 50. In the study area land under cultivation of food crops is gradually getting switched over to cultivation of non-food crops as evidenced by trend lines obtained with the software package SMART

casuarina plantations were successfully raised earlier, are now found abandoned.

f) Cultivation of ragi and millets has completely stopped because of lack of water. In fields under groundnut, the number of pods from each plant when compared with the past has lessened significantly.

g) Even when there is good rain the moisture does not remain in the soil for long but is either quickly drained underground or runs-off to the sea due to the barenness of the land in many places.

h) In recent years, for the benefit of the farmers, the Panchayat has dug well-like structures so that rain water is collected in them for use in irrigation. This water is being mainly used to irrigate non-food crops like casuarina as most of the farmers have switched over from food crops to non-food crops. Even these wells actually retain very little water and that too is getting polluted by the run-off from the solid wastes dumped by the industries in the vicinity of these wells. As a result the total area under *irrigated* non-food crops (Figure 51) has sharply declined and is gradually getting converted to either non-irrigated (rainfed) area or fallow lands (Figure 52).

i) The land-use is rapidly shifting away from agriculture-dominated one wheras agriculture is still dominant in the control area (Figure 53). As agricultural lands in Pillayarkuppam - Kirumampakkam have gradually become unproductive the farmers have either sold them to industries or to other commercial agencies.

j) The total available land for miscellaneous trees and groves which was almost 130 hectares in 1990 has come down to very few acres by 1991 (Figure 54).

k) In the coconut farm at Kirumampakkam behind Pondicherry Papers Limited (PPL), the coconut saplings planted a few years ago show insignificant growth. Most of the saplings are getting dried and have started disappearing. The farm is almost bare with only a few saplings still surviving and they too are not showing any signs of normal growth. During rains

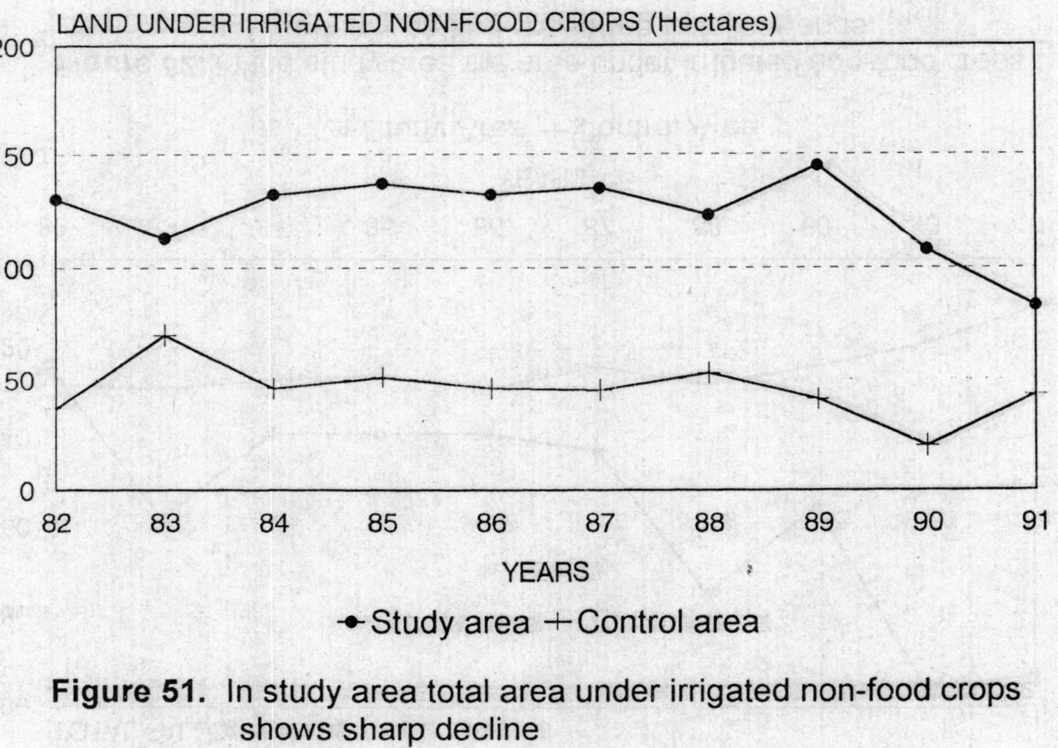

Figure 51. In study area total area under irrigated non-food crops shows sharp decline

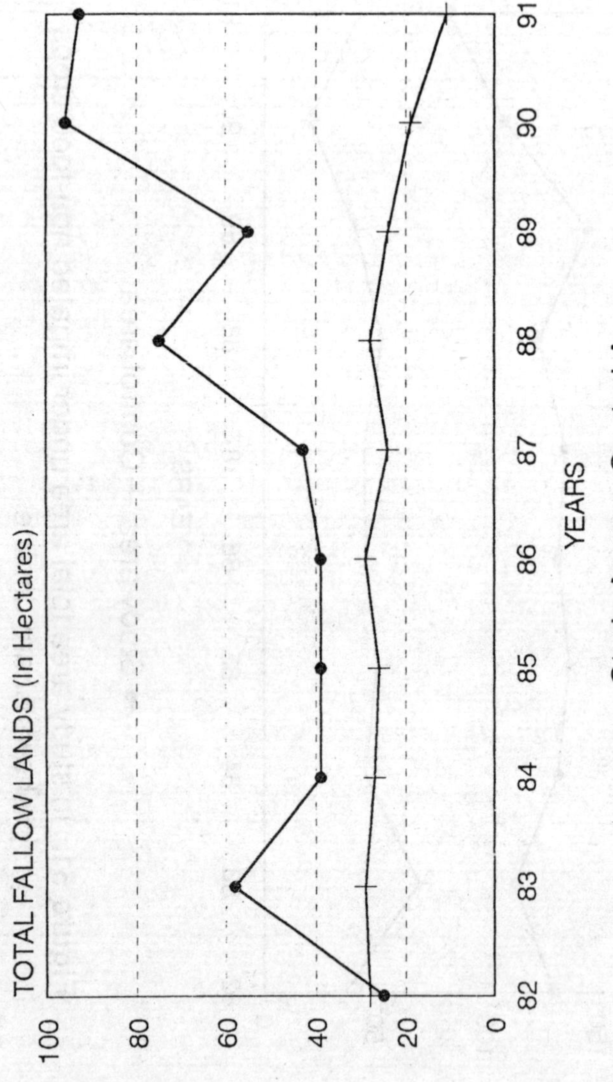

Figure 52. In the study area the area under irrigated non-food crops are gradually getting converted to fallow lands

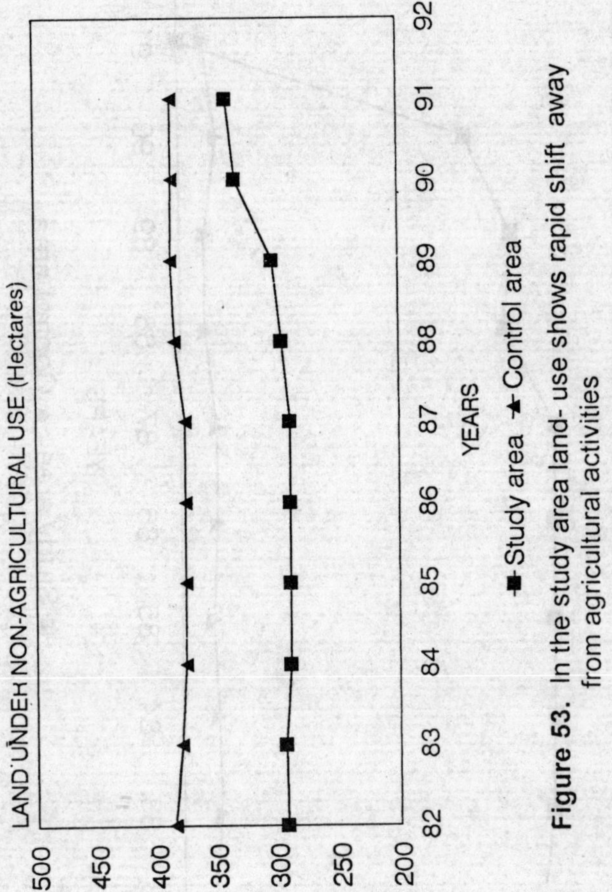

Figure 53. In the study area land- use shows rapid shift away from agricultural activities

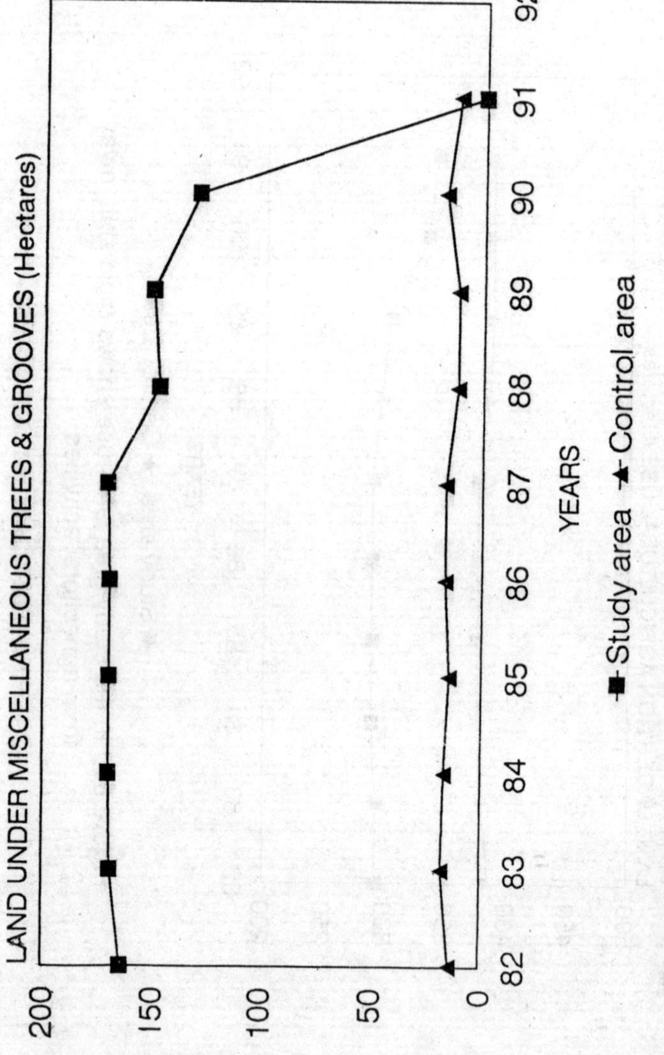

Figure 54. In the study area land available for miscellaneous trees and grooves is sharply declining

the effluents from the PPL overflow and pass through this farm to the adjacent low-lying area. At the same time the adjacent farm which was also planted with coconut during the same period but which has been away from the path of the PPL's effluent flow, has its trees growing normally, even bearing fruits.

These findings clearly depict the present status of the agricultural practices and of the degradation in land quality of the study area.

A drastic shift is noticed from agriculture dominated activities to other commercial developments. This change in land-use as compared to the pre-industrialisation period and the out come of the survey conducted among the large number of locals, as well as the declining trend noticed in various agriculture related activities as compared to the past 10 years data, reveals that the scarcity of adequate quantity of surface/ground water resources and the lose in the fertility of the agricultural land as the most likely causes for the present deteriorated state of the land environment.

Impact of Solid Waste Dumps

The results of the soild waste leachate study, summarized in Table 3.34, indicate that the leachate is thick with toxic metals mercury, arsenic, and cadmium; besides manganese and iron. The concentration of these metals in the leachate are found to be far exceeding the safe limits. The most toxic of these metals, mercury, is present at concentrations 70 to 500 times the permissible limit in the leachate. In most of the cases, the limits for iron, arsenic and cadmium are seen exceeded both for irrigation and drinking water. Manganese is present at levels higher than the limit for drinking water in all the cases and is even found at concentrations exceeding the limit for irrigation water in one case.

In terms of environmental pollution the damage due to solid wastes is being caused in several ways as summarized below.

a) The wastes, having been put in an unconfined space, get scattered due to the action of water and wind thus poisoning much larger tracts of land than are directly polluted due to the dump.

Table 3.34 : Characteristics of the solid waste leachate

		Sample A		*Sample B*	
S.No.	*Parameter*	*0.5 hrs*	*24 hrs.*	*0.5 hrs*	*24 hrs.*
1.	pH	8.03	8.03	7.77	7.91
2.	EC (μ mho/cm)	247.5	305.00	414.8	530.7
3.	Hardness ($mgCaCO_3/l$)	160.0	216.0	184.0	168.0
4.	Alkalinity ($mgCaCO_3/l$)	96.0	79.0	16.0	14.0
5.	Arsenic (mg/l)	0.503	0.251	0.314	0.125
6.	Cadmium (mg/l)	0.082	0.077	0.082	0.077
7.	Zinc (mg/l)	0.121	0.126	0.178	0.115
8.	Mercury (mg/l)	0.079	0.184	0.053	0.525
9.	Manganese (mg/l)	0.307	0.161	0.128	0.074
10.	Iron (mg/l)	2.057	17.26	1.092	2.137
11.	Nickel (mg/l)	0.020	0.020	0.020	0.020

b) During rains, soluble pollutants are leached out from the waste piles. When the leachate-bearing water percolates through the soil it contaminates it all the way down and through to the groundwater table.

c) Solid waste contaminates the nearby vegetation—as indeed distant vegetation when it gets scattered. When cattle graze on such vegetation the pollutants contaminate them and through them reach humans. Due to scarcity of sweet water caused by salinity intrusion (which is, in turn, hastened by overuse of groundwater by industries, and pollution) people living in the area use the existing ponds for bathing and fishing. This becomes another serious avenue for the pollutants to reach humans. The impact of such pollutants can be particularly severe on children.

4 Summary and Conclusions

1. All (100%) of the samples taken in the sensitive area, during the day as well as night, in the three seasons of Winter, Summer and Monsoon were polluted.

2. At PIPDIC industrial estate, as many as 86% and 50% of the day samples taken during March 1994 and January 1995 respectively and 100% and 60% of the night samples during March 1994 and June-October 1994 respectively were polluted. The percentage of polluted samples with other months ranged from 10% to 40% during the day and 40% to 50% during the night.

3. At resident I upto 80% of the day samples and 100% of the night samples taken during February 1995 were polluted. Even in other months the percentage of polluted samples ranged from 13% to 60% during the day and 40% to 86% during the night.

4. At residential II upto 100% of the day and night samples taken during February 1994 indicated unacceptable air quality. In the same site 60% and 20% of the day samples and 80% and 60% taken during March - April 1994 respectively were polluted.

5. In the local Residential III 20% of the day samples and 60% of the night samples were found polluted.

6. In no locality less than 10% of the day samples and 40% of the night samples taken in any month were free from pollution.

7. It was observed that in all the samples the electrical conductivity exceeded the drinking water standards.

8. Alkalinity was found to be surpassing the permissible limit in most cases.

9. Hardness surpassed the permissible limits for drinking water in 79% of the surface water samples and 72% of the ground water samples.

10. Sulphate is also found to be in excess of the limit for drinking water - both for surface water and ground water.

11. The phosphorous content of the ground water and surface water exceeded the limits for domestic water in 89% and 63% of cases respectively.

12. For 79% of the samples the BOD is exceeding the limits for domestic water.

13. In 100% of the surface water samples total suspended solids (TSS) were above the permissible level during the monsoon and post monsoon periods.

14. Mercury was found in concentrations 150 to 1100 times higher than the permissible limit for drinking water.

15. The concentration of arsenic, mercury, iron, manganese and cadmium was found to be crossing the permissible levels for drinking water in 100% cases. Arsenic, cadmium and maganese (for surface water) were also found to be present at levels higher than allowable for irrigation water in 100% cases.

16. Land use studies and survey of flora indicate that the species diversity is poor and now only a few hardy and tolerant plants dominate the region.

17. A drastic shift is noticed from agriculture dominated activities to other commercial developments. There is a decline in both agricultural crop productivity and quality.

18. It is also noticed that in all the stages the control area shows almost a regular and constant trend in the agricultural activities for the past 10 years when compared to the study area.

19. The results of the solid waste leachate analysis indicate that the leachate is thick with toxic metals like mercury, arsenic and cadmium ; besides manganese and Iron. The concentration of these metals in the leachate are found to be far exceeding the safe limit.

It is clearly brought out by the findings of this EIA, summarised in the preceeding pages, that the air, water, land as well as the biotic environment of Pillayarkuppam - Kirumampakkam area has already become *grossly polluted*. The pollutant levels, recommended as acceptable by the regulatory agencies, are being repeatedly exceeded in the air as well as water - with consequent and drastically adverse impact on the biotic environment.

It is therefore clear that :

a) *No such new industry that has gaseous, aqueous, or solid emissions may be permitted in the area nor permission for capacity expansion be granted to any such industry* unless strong and swift steps are taken for bringing down pollutant emission levels and restoring the water and land environments. Only non-polluting (green category) industries may be permitted as of now.

b) In order that the ambient air and water pollution levels in the area are brought down to within permissible levels it is imperative that the pollution control measures thus far adopted by each of the industries are reviewed and suitably upgraded. *It must be ensured that the sum total contribution by all the industries to environmental contamination in the area is brought within the acceptable levels.*

c) The disposal of liquid and solid effluents on land must be stopped forthwith. The effluents should be properly treated and *unauthorised letting out of these effluents in the surface water bodies should be firmly checked.* Similarly the solid wastes should be properly treated and *must not be dumped on land or in water.*

d) Development of green belt around each industry should be made mandatory so as to improve the microclimate of the area and provide receptors for some of the pollutants.

e) Since salinity intrusion has already taken place in alarming proportions, *overexploitation of ground water must be stopped forthwith* and the Central Pollution Control Board norms preventing digging of borewells within close proximity to the coast should be strictly followed. Industries should meet their water requirements primarily through recycling after treatment of polluted water.

This work has highlighted the degree of degradation in the environmental quality brought about by unplanned industrialisation in the rural Pillayarkuppam - Kirumampakkam industrial areas. Immediate measures from the government and the industries coupled with public consciousness and participation, has to be stressed upon at this juncture. All the objectives, as envisaged at the time of initiation of this work have been fulfilled. Therefore, this data can serve as a substrate for further research, leading towards significant conclusions.

Annexures

ANNEXURE - I

Maximum permissible levels of SPM, NO_x and SO_2 as per Central Pollution Control Board Standards

Sl.No.	*Type of Area*	*SPM ($\mu g/Nm^3$)*	*No_x ($\mu g/Nm^3$)*	*SO_2 ($\mu g/Nm^3$)*
1.	Industrial	500	120	120
2.	Residential/general	200	80	80
3.	Sensitive	100	30	30

ANNEXURE - II

Water Quality Standards

Sl.No.	*Parameters*	*Standards for Drinking Water*	*Standards for Domestic Water*	*Standards for Irrigation Water*
1.	pH	6.5-8.5	6.0-9.0	--
2.	EC (μ mho/cm^3)	--	300.0	--
3.	TSS (mg/l)	--	5.0	--
4.	TDS (mg/l)	500.0	500	--

Contd.

ANNEXURE - II (contd.)

Water Quality Standards

Sl.No.	*Parameters*	*Standards for Drinking Water*	*Standards for Domestic Water*	*Standards for Irrigation Water*
5.	Acidity (mg $CaCo_3$/l)	--	--	--
6.	Alkalinity (mg $CaCo_3$/l)	200.0	--	--
7.	Hardness (mg $CaCo_3$/l)	300.0	--	--
8.	Chloride (mg cl/l)	250.0	600.0	--
9.	Salinity (mg Nacl/l)	250.0	600.0	--
10.	Nitrogen (Total) (mg/l)	--	-	-
11.	Phosphorus (mg Po_4/l)	-	0.1	-
12.	Sulphate (mg So_4/l)	200.0	1000.0	-
13.	Do (mg/l)	-	3.0	-
14.	BOD (mg/l)	-	3.0	-
15.	COD (mg/l)	-	-	-
16.	Iron (mg/l)	0.3	-	5.0
17.	Mercury (mg/l)	0.001	-	-
18.	Cadmium (mg/l)	0.01	-	0.01
19.	Arsenic (mg/l)	0.05	-	0.10
20.	Zinc (mg/l)	5	-	2.0
21.	Manganese (mg/l)	0.1	-	0.20
22.	Nickel (mg/l)	-	-	0.20

ANNEXURE - III.

Correlation Coefficient of Surface Water

	pH	EC	TSS	TDS	Acidity	Alkali-nity	Hard-ness	Chloride	Salinity	Nitro-gen	Phospho-rous	Sulphate	DO	BOD	COD
pH	1	.603	.138	.484	.406	.414	.512	.363	.352	.228	.281	.447	.378	.390	.411
EC		1	.161	.613	.173	.541	.681	.539	.286	.114	.446	.245	.201	.305	.158
TSS			1	.122	.498	.285	.089	.114	.152	.105	.02	.138	.063	.118	.240
TDS				1	.176	.422	.752	.703	.681	.184	.318	.265	.329	.379	.288
Acidity					1	.361	.421	.341	.355	.095	.379	.475	.184	.055	.014
Alkalinity						1	.612	.595	.654	.387	.367	.032	.326	.471	.032
Hardness							1	.807	.816	.219	.556	.572	.158	.122	.095
Chloride								1	.982	.231	.541	.404	.235	.332	.247
Salinity									1	.179	.533	.380	.237	.375	.182
Nitrogen										1	.155	.550	.02	.494	.105
Phosphorous											1	.322	.158	.155	.032
Sulphate												1	.374	.217	.0007
DO													1	.221	.045
BOD														1	.6
COD															1

ANNEXURE - IV.

Correlation Coefficient of Ground Water

	pH	EC	TSS	TDS	Acidity	Alkalinity	Hardness	Chloride	Salinity	Nitrogen	Phosphorous	Sulphate	DO	BOD	COD
pH	1	.555	.084	.612	.472	.523		.575	.375	.370	.410	.192		.540	.265
EC		1	.110	.410	.277	.699		.711	.573	.620	.510	.071		.675	.253
TSS			1	0.0	.230	.176		.148	.221	.247	.358	.095		.09	.155
TDS				1	.071	.411		.511	.266	.219	.302	.356		.326	.321
Acidity					1	.315		.374	.429	.371	.032	.101		.486	.063
Alkalinity						1		.701	.345	.315	.348	.130		.643	.207
Hardness							1		.642	.611	.322	.195		.854	.270
Chloride									1	.939	.032	.471		.791	.329
Salinity										1	.02	.496		.776	.468
Nitrogen											1	.024		.155	.1
Phosphorous												1		.281	.863
Sulphate													1		.345
COD															1

Bibliography

Abbasi,S.A. (1995). *Experimental Aquatic Ecology And Water Pollution*, Vol 1, Pondicherry (central) University, Pondicherry, India.

American Public Health Association (cited as APHA) (1977). *Methods of air sampling and analysis*, 2nd ed. Washington, D.C: 984 pages.

American Public Health Association (cited as APHA) (1992). *Standard Methods for the Estimation of water and wastewater.* 18th ed. Washington, D.C:pp.6-187.

Barbara, A. and Harry, I. (1980). Relationships between ground water Silica, Total Dissolved Solids and Specific Electrical Conductivity. *Journal of Ground water*, **22** (1), pp.80.

Battan, L.J. (1979). *Fundamentals of Meteorology*. Prentice Hall, Engle wood cliffs, N.J.

Council of environmental quality (1982). *Twelth annual report of the council of the environmental quality.* Washington, D.C.

Dhanaselvan,M.C.K. and Perumalsamy,L. (1991). Physico chemical contamination of well water of Kanpur city. *Indian J.Environ. Prot*, 11(2),pp. 133-139.

Indian Standard (IS: 2490) (1981). *Domestic water specification.* Bureau of Indian Standards, New Delhi, India.

Indian Standard (IS: 10500) (1993). *Drinking water specification.* Bureau of Indian Standards, New Delhi, India.

Indian Standard (IS: 2296). *Methods of sampling and test (physical and chemical) for water and waste water.* Bureau of Indian Standards, New Delhi, India.

Indian Standard (IS: 2488) *Methods of sampling and test (Physical and chemical) for water and waste water.* Bureau of Indian standards, New Delhi, India.

Institute for air pollution training (1975). *Air pollutants and their sources.* In air pollution control orientation course (422-A), U.S., EPA. Atlanta.

Manual for statistical analysis and interpretation of water quality data (1987). Central board for the prevention and control of water pollution, New Delhi, India: 151 pages.

Mathew, G.(1982). *The properties of Ground water.* John Wiley and Sons, New York: 406 pages.

Olaniya, M.S., Sayena, K.L. and Bharagava, R.K. (1969). Well water quality in Jaipur city. *Env. Health*, Vol.II, pp. 378-391.

Peavy,G.H., Rowe, R.D. and Tchobanoglous, G. (1986). *Environmental Engineering.* MCGraw - Hill Book Co., pp.417-513.

Ramesh,N.B., Srikanth,R. and Rao, M.A. (1993). Ambient NO_x,SO_x and SPM levels in the Industrial, Commercial and Residential Areas of Hyderabad city. *Poll. Res.*, 12 (4), pp.239-243.

Ravindra, P.(1991). Studies on suspended particulate matter in an industrial area. *Indian J.Environ. Prot.*, 11 (5), pp.358-359.

Razia,S., Prakash, S.P.K., Ramesh, N.B. and Raza, S.H. (1990). Ground water quality of Nacharam industrial complex. *Acta Ecologia*, 12 (2), pp.119-124.

Singh,C., Parwana, H.K., Singh, R.S. and Marwaha, S.S. (1994). Suspended particulate matter and SO_2 emissions from Guru Gobind Singh Thermal Plant, Ropar (Punjab). *Poll. Res.*, 13(1),pp. 79-81.

Stern, A.C., Henry, C.W., Richard, W.D. and William, P.L. (1973). *Fundamentals of air pollution*. Acadamic press, New York.

Subba Rao, N. (1993). Environmental impact of industrial effluents in ground water regime of Vishakapatnam industrial complex. *Indian J.Geo.*, **65** (1), pp.35-43.

Subramanian, V. (1989). Impact of industrial development on environment and ecosystem. *Proc. (vol.2), 10th Ann. Sess. Acad. Environ. Bio. & Semin. Environ. Impact Biosystems*, Loyola college, Madras, Tamil Nadu, India:pp.39-45.

[illegible] Heine, C.W., [illegible] W.T. and Wilson, [illegible] (19[illegible]). [illegible] Academic Press, New York.

Sastry, Rao, M. (199[illegible]). Environmental impact of industrial [illegible] [illegible] Indian J. [illegible] (5): [illegible] 25-43.

Srivastava, V. (1989). Impact of industrial development on environment and ecosystem [illegible] [illegible] [illegible] Impact Assessment, [illegible] New Delhi, India, 1989.